WILEY

FASTCOMPANY

READER SERIES

BUSINESS ETHICS

WILEY
FASTCOMPANY
READER SERIES

PATRICK E. MURPHY, EDITOR

University of Notre Dame

www.wiley.com/college/murphy

To
Past, present, and future ethical businesspeople:
May their character and integrity enlighten others

Acquisitions Editor   *Jeff Marshall*
Marketing Manager   *Charity Robey*
Editorial Assistant   *Jessica Bartelt*
Managing Editor   *Lari Bishop*
Associate Production Manager   *Kelly Tavares*
Production Editor   *Sarah Wolfman-Robichaud*
Designer   *Jaye Joseph*
Cover Design   *Richard Pacifico*

This book was set in 10/12 Garamond by Leyh Publishing LLC and printed and bound by Courier Corporation. The cover was printed by Phoenix Color Corp.

This book is printed on acid free paper. ∞

ISBN: 0-471-44462-6

Printed in the United States of America

10   9   8   7   6   5   4   3   2   1

CONTENTS

SECTION 1: AN OVERVIEW OF BUSINESS ETHICS　　9

SECTION 2: THE ENRON DEBACLE　　23

A Monthly Column on Strategy

The Secret Life of the CEO: Do They Even Know Right from Wrong?

SECTION 6: BUSINESS ETHICS EARLY IN THE 21ST CENTURY 131

Five Half-Truths of Business

Can You Keep a Secret?

Global Values in a Local World

Good Work

ACKNOWLEDGEMENTS

No book-length manuscript is the product of one person. I would like to acknowledge the assistance of several individuals who helped make this publication possible. First, the authors of the *Fast Company* articles included in this anthology deserve recognition for crafting the original articles. Furthermore, a recent editorial by the founder indicates some aspects of the magazine that have changed since it was introduced in 1995, and what hasn't changed. Here is an excerpt reflecting *Fast Company's* commitment to ethical and socially responsible business:

> … we stand for something. In the battle of ideas, *Fast Company* is not neutral. We are the magazine for business leaders who are looking to bring out the best in themselves—the magazine for companies that believe that you win by doing what's right, not what you can get away with.

At the University of Notre Dame, there are several people that deserve special thanks. First, Carolyn Woo, Dean of the Mendoza College of Business, provides leadership, commitment, and support for those of us working in business ethics. Second, Joe Guiltinan, the Chair of the Department of Marketing, has allowed me to concentrate my teaching and research in the areas of business and marketing ethics. Third, Tom Klein, my colleague, provided several helpful editorial suggestions for the opening essay. Fourth, Monica Smith and Diana Laquinta, my student assistants, helped move the project forward in several ways. Finally, and most significantly, Deb Coch, who serves as my administrative assistant, conscientiously and patiently worked through the multiple drafts of the manuscript.

At John Wiley and Sons, Jeff Marshall, former editor for Management and Marketing, deserves credit for proposing the idea of this reader. His view that it would be useful as a supplement to many existing courses—whether they be in ethics, business and society, or other functional areas of business—is sound. Jeff, thanks for the opportunity to assemble this text. His successor, Jessica Bartelt, saw the project through to its completion.

Finally, I want to thank my family for their continuing support over the years. Kate, my wife of twenty-five years, has given the love and reinforcement that has sustained me during my academic career. Our three wonderful sons, Bob, Brendan, and Jim, have provided us many joys of parenthood. Thanks to all of you for being there.

Despite the assistance of all these people, I accept full responsibility for any errors that remain in the text. Happy reading to all.

Patrick E. Murphy
Notre Dame, Indiana
November 2002

ABOUT THE EDITOR

PATRICK E. MURPHY

Patrick E. Murphy is Professor of Marketing and the C.R. Smith Director of the Institute for Ethical Business Worldwide in the Mendoza College of Business at the University of Notre Dame. Professor Murphy recently completed a ten year term as Chair of the Department of Marketing. Previously, Professor Murphy served on the faculty at Marquette University for nine years. He is a former editor of the *Journal of Public Policy & Marketing* and serves on the editorial board of four journals. He holds a Ph.D. from the University of Houston, an M.B.A. from Bradley University and a B.B.A. from Notre Dame.

He has written a number of scholarly articles on business and marketing ethics. His book, *Eighty Exemplary Ethics Statements*, is published by the Notre Dame Press (1998). Gene Laczniak and he are co-authors of *Ethical Marketing Decisions: The Higher Road* (Prentice Hall, 1993) and the book is currently under revision. He is a member of the Advisory Board for *Annual Editions: Business Ethics*. His articles and cases have won awards from the *Journal of Macromarketing* and the European Case Clearing House.

Professor Murphy received the 1992 Reinhold Niebuhr Award given annually to one faculty member at the University of Notre Dame whose writings promote the areas of ethics and social justice. He was a Fulbright Scholar in the Department of Management and Marketing at University College Cork in Ireland in 1993–94. Murphy was recognized in 1997 as one of the "Top Researchers in Marketing" for sustained contribution to the field. Professor Murphy received a 2001 Special Presidential Award from Notre Dame. In 2002, he was the recipient of a Kaneb Award for Undergraduate Teaching and appointed as an Invited Fellow of the Ethics Resource Center in Washington, DC.

He has held several recent leadership positions in professional association conferences. In 1998, he was conference co-chair of the Marketing Exchange Colloquia in Vienna, Austria. In 1999, he was co-chair of the Marketing and Public Policy Conference and organizer of the Symposium on Teaching Ethics in Marketing both held at Notre Dame. In 2000, he served as the conference co-chair for the AMA Summer Educators' Conference. Murphy and Gene Laczniak organized a special workshop for the American Marketing Association on Teaching Marketing Ethics in 2003.

Professor Murphy resides with his wife, Kate, and three sons, Bob, Brendan and Jim, in Granger, Indiana.

INTRODUCTION

As this book is being completed late in the year 2002, the last twelve months have seen business issues move from the business section of newspapers and magazines to the front page. Unfortunately, most of these front-page stories have chronicled violations of business ethics and shortcomings in corporate governance. The Enron fiasco (featured in Section 2 of the book) was the initial scandal that rocked corporate America. The bankruptcy of the then seventh largest company in the United States caused everyone to take notice. Of course, the accounting firm of Arther Andersen was implicated in the Enron scandal and was the first to be indicted. As we now know, this firm has basically ceased to operate. Additional major ethical violations were reported at Adelphia, Merrill Lynch, Tyco, WorldCom, and Martha Stewart (the person and the brand). Although no new scandals have arisen in the last several months, the languishing stock market and lack of trust in corporate America remain a testament to these major ethical violations.

RECENT ETHICAL AND CORPORATE RESPONSIBILITY ISSUES

CEO/Executive Pay and Performance

Responsibility for the scandals mentioned all fall at the doorstep of the chief executive or top management team. Many argue that the individuals involved have demonstrated ethical egoism rather than their fiduciary duty in running their respective corporations. Individual greed, winning at all costs, and pumping up the stock price by any means have been given as reasons a number of these managers displayed such a lack of ethical consciousness. However, some critics believe the phenomenal pay levels of top executives have led to the "imperial" corporate executive or a superstar mentality. Once these individuals have such a view of themselves, it is not surprising that their behavior may breach generally accepted ethical precepts. Furthermore, many of the lower-level executives in these firms obviously did not want to bring bad news to the CEO. In the fifth section of this anthology, we use several *Fast Company* articles to indicate remedies for the present situation regarding some CEOs.

Boards of Directors' Responsibilities

The role of boards of directors appears to have changed in recent years from one of being accountable to the shareholders to being captive, in some instances, of top management. The objectivity of board members has been questioned, as well as their ties to the firm. "Independent" board members seem to be less and less common today. The Enron board (although not discussed in the articles to follow) was especially susceptible to these criticisms in that several of the board members were consultants to Enron or executives of organizations that received money from Enron. In addition, some had political ties to the corporation. When a board suspends its ethics code, like the Enron board did on two occasions, it is highly doubtful they are discharging their duties to shareholders, let alone to other stakeholders.

Conflicts of Interest of Accounting Firms and Investment Analysts

The conflicts these organizations experienced in relation to their dealings with both corporations and the investment community is well documented. One article in this anthology discusses management consultants' ethical shortcomings. The obvious conflicts between selling consulting services as well as audit services to large corporations like Enron and WorldCom seemed to be evident to many outside observers, but to few in the actual profession. Similarly, the investment analysts' reluctance to objectively analyze stocks on which they were reporting caused similar problems. This issue is examined in the Enron section that follows. The negative publicity, in addition to the monetary loss in a number of these firms, led to not only a chastened outlook but also to a much more vigilant approach to business. Furthermore, regulatory mechanisms are playing a much stronger role than in recent years. This moves us to the final point in this section.

Regulation

The Congressional testimony of many Enron executives and employees dominated the news in mid-2002. A lack of clearly expressed motives for the behavior of many Enron top managers, as well as the sympathetic view toward employees and pensioners who lost virtually all their savings, caused Congress to act. The Sarbanes-Oxley Act was passed on July 30, 2002. This law requires both the CEO and CFO to sign off on the financial documents of their firms. If these numbers should prove to be false or inflated, the top executives can be held criminally responsible. (The original text of the Sarbanes-Oxley Act can be found at http://findlaw.com; for a summary and strengths and weaknesses see www.aicpa.org/info/sarbanes_oxley_summary.htm and Baue 2002).

In addition to this legislation, the Securities and Exchange Commission (SEC) became a much more active regulator of corporate America. Congress voted for a major increase in funding for the SEC. Former SEC chairman, Harvey L. Pitt, resigned after coming under attack from many parties. Initially, the criticism was based on his past ties to the accounting profession, and then on his handling of a new board to oversee the accounting profession. The chair of the SEC in the former administration, Arthur Levitt, has been very critical of an accounting firm offering both consulting as well as auditing services to the same client. Most of his criticisms have been vindicated at this point. He is the author of a new book that examines this area in depth (Levitt and Dwyer 2002).

Corporate Responses

One should be mindful that the scandals we have discussed were concentrated in a dozen or so major corporations. Most companies and their top executives seek to promote ethical behavior in their dealings with stakeholders. These firms use a variety of mechanisms to ensure that employees follow ethical guidelines in their day-to-day business dealings. There are four such programmatic approaches that corporations use: compliance, values/integrity, social outreach, and privacy.

Over 90 percent of large U.S.-based companies currently have a code of ethics (Murphy 1998). The Sarbanes-Oxley Act requires other firms to promulgate codes in the near future. Codes are usually longer and more legalistic type documents. They can range in length from a few pages to over one hundred pages. Compliance programs ask employees to follow the rules. Large multinationals with thousands of employees are required to have a code of ethics because of their far-flung operations. Many employees may not be familiar with the top management stance towards ethics. Among the companies with exemplary codes of ethics are Boeing, Caterpillar, Guardsmark, and United Technologies.

The values/integrity approach begins with a relatively short corporate values statement rather than a longer code. It can be contrasted with the code in that values tell employees what to "do" while compliance programs provide a "don't" list. Compliance codes of ethics are administered by the Legal Department where the values/integrity programs tend to be the domain of either the Ethics Officer or the Human Resources Department. In fact, the Ethics Officer Association has over eight hundred members (www.eoa.org), mostly from the largest corporations in the United States.

Values statements tend to be a list of corporate principles that range in number from three to ten (Murphy 1998). They are often communicated through promotional information, small cards, framed in offices, and annual reports. The third type of ethics statement that is also under the jurisdiction of a values/integrity program is a corporate credo. The Johnson and Johnson Credo, developed in the 1940's, is the best-known example. J & J has translated the Credo into more than fifty languages for use around the world. Credos tend to list the responsibilities or obligations of the company to its various stakeholders.

A number of large corporations, who start with a compliance/code program, eventually move to an integrity or values approach. They realize having rules is not enough. Therefore, some of the most progressive organizations have both codes and values statements. The emphasis then becomes integrity rather than just following the rules laid out in the code of ethics. In fact, General Electric calls its ethics program an "integrity" initiative, even though it has aspects of compliance in it.

Another type of ethics program, which is not mutually exclusive from the other two, is focused on social outreach (Donaldson 2000). A social outreach program emphasizes the company's role as a citizen. This approach is either one of social accounting or social responsibility. A growing number of companies, such as P&G and Shell, report on what they call a triple bottom line, which includes the economic, social, and environmental aspects of their operations. Other companies, such as

Merck, have developed products that they made available to third-world consumers. The Mectizan drug, which cured river blindness, is an excellent and well-cited example of this type of initiative (Bollier 1991). Corporate citizenship is receiving more attention (Goodpaster 2001) and includes the responsibility to the firm's mission as well as a social responsibility component. Executive responsibility must be placed on top management to ensure the vision becomes reality.

Social outreach or corporate citizenship programs are not sufficient to be considered a highly ethical corporation. The best example is Enron, which had a plethora of community-based programs supporting the arts, Enron Field, and other social causes in the Houston area. In fact, the firm won a number of environmental awards, innovative company awards, as well as being one of the most admired corporations in the year 2000. One observer's assessment on these Enron activities regarding corporate citizenship is "fluff is not enough" (Waddock 2002). All of these corporate giving programs and awards and recognition amount to nothing if the company's practices are not aligned with the company's stated values and daily operating practices. Therefore, the media and other corporate watchdogs need to be more questioning about future social outreach programs.

The final response that corporations have made regarding ethical issues refers to privacy statements. These statements, which usually deal with Internet-based communications, let consumers know the level of privacy they might expect from each corporation. Legislation currently exists forcing financial institutions to communicate their policy statements to consumers (but not other industries).

As in the case of compliance programs, the legal interpretation of privacy is one that often carries the day. The best privacy policies explain in plain English whether the firm is going to utilize cookies, collect personal information, and share it with other individuals. One article in the final section of this book makes several excellent points that any organization should use in developing or revising its privacy statement. Companies should strive for an ethical, rather than legal, privacy position, not only with consumers, but also with employees and other important stakeholders.

BUSINESS ETHICS IN THE FUTURE

This author believes four areas are essential to improving ethical decision making within corporations at this time. The first is ethical leadership. Despite the scandals of the last year, the emphasis on top managers, especially the CEO, who epitomize the ethical values of the organization, cannot be overstated. There are many examples in the business world today. In fact, *Business Week* recently ran a cover story on five good CEOs (Byrne 2002), and a Harvard professor, Lynn Paine (2003), discussed ethical leadership displayed by AES executives (featured in this reader) and several other firms in her book. The corporate leader and the top management team can make a huge difference in how well a corporation succeeds in fulfilling its ethical responsibilities.

A second area is the growing importance of transparency and vigilance within corporations, and with their boards and auditors. During the discussion of the recent scandals, observers have indicated that many of the financial statements of these organizations were not transparent. Companies that highlight transparency have much less difficulty with ethical problems, given that they are willing to share information with their stakeholders. The concept of "open book" management, popularized by Jack Stack, is now being endorsed by more firms (Case 1995; Stack 1994; Stack and Burlingham 2002).

Vigilance, especially by boards of directors and auditing firms, seems to be a watchword of the first decade of the 21st century. Several boards, especially Enron's, have been criticized for being "asleep at the switch." Although legislation has been passed to police many of the problems that have emerged regarding financial disclosures, some companies will undoubtedly try to cheat in the future. It is incumbent, then, on the board members and auditors to take their role as watchdogs much more seriously than in the past. This writer would encourage readers to implement the "ethic of the mean" as it relates to both transparency and vigilance. The objective of firms and individuals is to strike a balance rather than going to extremes in practicing transparency and vigilance.

The third compelling area is recognition of conflicts of interest. Many of the scandals occurred because one or more of the major players did not recognize the conflict of interest. Besides the high-level executives at these companies, investment banks and their research, brokerage, and IPO arms, as well as accounting firms with consulting and auditing practices, were rife with conflicts of interest. Although much has now been changed by legislation or company policy, this does not mean that conflicts of interest are totally behind us. Executives always have a conflict between their duties to shareholders and other stakeholders. The recognition and balancing of these various ethical responsibilities continue to be major potential problem areas for companies in the foreseeable future. One might argue that boards of directors and ethics officers and auditors should stand ready to help top executives in dealing with conflicts of interest. However, the first stage is the recognition of the problem. Unfortunately, recognition of ethical transgressions is still not as high as it should be.

A fourth area needing greater emphasis is moral imagination. This term has been defined by Johnson (1993) as: "an ability to imaginatively discern various possibilities for acting within a given situation and to envision the potential help and harm that are likely to result from a given action" (202). The increasingly complex ethical problems facing all firms, whether multinational or small entrepreneurial ventures, require greater insight and "outside the box" thinking. This writer is certainly not advocating being imaginative in a negative moral sense. What we need is more creative thinking so that growing ethical and social problems receive greater attention and emphasis. For example, Binney and Smith's (the makers of Crayola Crayons) corporate values include the following: "Think outside the lines: challenge and encourage others to do so as well."

Moral imagination can be combined with ethical decision making (Werhane 1999). She said: "it is a dynamic process, which challenges the presuppositions of tradition, tests one's impartiality against context, and continues to shape one's decisions and refine one's moral standards" (126). Moral imagination must be cultivated and nurtured on the part of all employees, and following Werhane's advice seems like a very good place to begin.

OUTLINE OF THE BOOK

This book is organized into five sections. Each contains several articles from *Fast Company* relating to some aspect of business ethics and social responsibility. An attempt was made to arrange the articles in such a manner that each section could be used as a self-contained unit. Certainly, some instructors will decide that they prefer a different order or to only assign some of the articles.

Section 1—An Overview of Business Ethics features three articles. The first examines the difficult task of rebuilding trust at eBay after the events of September 11, 2001. Second, an interview with an expert on professional services that advances the assumption that many consultants are corrupt. Finally, "new rules" for dealing with customers are discussed based on selections from a recent book. These rules have to do with honesty, fairness, and respect for the consumer.

Section 2—The Enron Debacle contains four articles. The May 2002 issue of *Fast Company* provided a comprehensive examination of the Enron bankruptcy and its aftermath. The first article discusses the views of several former Enron employees. The role of Wall Street in the Enron affair is chronicled in the second article. The last two articles focus on the future: how to spot another Enron in the future and what the world will look like after Enron.

Section 3—Social Responsibility examines the social role of three organizations. Both a U.S.-based (Interface) and a South African (Freeplay Group) firm are profiled in the separate articles. A not-for-profit organization (Pioneer Human Services) is discussed in the third article. The social responsibility of these organizations spans environmental issues, hiring the disabled, and providing jobs for former criminal offenders and drug addicts.

Section 4—Exemplary Companies includes four articles. AES, a multinational power company headquartered in Virginia, is the subject of the first article. The ethical posture of the firm and its founders is legendary. Lego, a familiar name to all of us, is the second company deemed exemplary. The firm's product line and its commitment to positive experiences for children are outstanding. St. Luke's, a London advertising agency, is profiled in the third article. This agency's egalitarian philosophy and its attention to both employees and customers distinguish it from almost all others in the advertising field. The final article discusses three firms who stress honesty in all actions.

Section 5—Ethical Business Leadership has five articles in it. A common understanding within business is that CEOs and top management set the ethical tone for the firm. The first article deals with women CEOs, the second profiles a specific CEO, while the third discusses the role mentoring plays in advancing a leader's career. These articles provide many insights into the important roles that CEOs can play in furthering the ethical posture of any corporation. The final two articles are more critical of CEO behavior and affirm that higher ethical responsibilities are needed in the future.

Section 6—Business Ethics Early in the 21st Century concludes the volume with four articles. The first focuses on business at the crossroads and dispels half-truths that companies have come to follow. Protection of personal privacy in the Internet age is the topic of the second article. A new weeklong seminar, "Core Values for a

Global Society," taught by a renowned philosopher is examined in the third article. Finally, the three co-authors of a book, *Good Work*, discuss their views on this subject. My hope for each reader is that you will find good work to challenge and reward you during your career.

REFERENCES

Baue, William. "The Strengths and Inadequacies of the Sarbanes-Oxley Act," at www.socialfunds.com/new /print.cgi?sfArticleId=936.

Bollier, David. "Merck & Co., Inc. (A)." *The Business Enterprise Trust* (1991).

Byrne, John A. "The Good CEO." *Business Week,* 23 September 2002, 80–88.

Case, J. *Open Book Management.* New York: Harper Collins Publishers, 1995.

Donaldson, Thomas. "Adding Corporate Ethics to the Bottom Line." *Financial Times,* 9 November 2000.

Goodpaster, Kenneth E. "Can a Corporation Be a Citizen?" *Defining a New Citizenship for South Africa,* 2001.

Johnson, Mark. *Moral Imagination.* Chicago: University of Chicago Press, 1993.

Levitt, Arthur and Paula Dwyer. *Take On the Street: What Wall Street and Corporate America Don't Want You to Know.* New York: Pantheon Books, 2002.

Murphy, Patrick E. *Eighty Exemplary Ethics Statements.* Notre Dame: University of Notre Dame Press, 1998.

Paine, Lynn. *Value Shift.* New York: McGraw-Hill, 2003.

Stack, Jack. *The Great Game of Business.* New York: Doubleday, 1994.

Stack, Jack, and B. Burlingham. *A Stake in the Outcome: Building a Culture of Ownership for the Long-Term Success of Your Business.* New York: Doubleday, 2002.

Waddock, Sandra. "Fluff Is Not Enough—Managing Responsibility for Corporate Citizenship." *Ethical Corporation Magazine,* 2 April 2002.

Werhane, Patricia H. *Moral Imagination and Management Decision Making.* New York: Oxford University Press, 1999.

AN OVERVIEW OF BUSINESS ETHICS

Each section of this book will begin with a brief introduction to the readings presented in the section. The three articles discussed here are "Business Fights Back: eBay Learns to Trust Again," "Are All Consultants Corrupt?" and "New Rules: Why Values Beat Value."

It seemed appropriate after the catastrophic events of September 11, 2001 to begin with an article that used this tragedy as a backdrop. The well-known company eBay is the subject of the first article, which discusses the company's quest to regain trust. This successful Internet company has two pillars of growth: the global spread of Internet-style capitalism and the confidence in the basic goodness of people who do business on the site. The article also uses Germany as a backdrop and the problems not too long ago associated with the Berlin Wall. The coming down of the Wall in 1989 affected business. This article has an optimistic tone to it and the bottom line is that eBay has not only survived, but has emerged from this major challenge as a stronger and better organization. The "Value of Good Works" also discusses some of the donations eBay made to the victims in New York, Washington, D.C., and Pennsylvania.

The second article has a decidedly different tone. In the wake of the Enron, Global Crossing, and WorldCom debacles, author Alan Webber asks the question: Are all consultants corrupt? Webber interviewed David Maister, who is an expert in studying professional services firms. He criticizes these companies for not practicing what they preach, as well as for following a minimalist compliance code. As the introductory section to this book pointed out, most highly ethical companies use a values or integrity approach to ethics. Many of these companies are too monetarily driven, and, even though they contend they are professionals, they are still concerned with the bottom line. Webber's admonition at the end of the article should be one that all employees of a professional service organization follow. He advocates that working with people who are shady or crooked is a recipe for disaster and knowledgeable employees should "get out!"

The third article contained in this short section is titled: "New Rules: Why Values Beat Value." This article also contains an interview with Ryan Mathews, coauthor of the recent book "The Myth of Excellence." He offers some surprising answers to customer satisfaction, and indicates that companies should forget the lowest price or the biggest discount. The watchwords for satisfying consumers are to show respect and tell the truth. In this era of cynicism toward business, these words of advice sound particularly appropriate.

BY GEORGE ANDERS   FROM *FAST COMPANY* ISSUE 53, PAGE 102

Business Fights Back: eBay Learns to Trust Again

THE WORLD'S MOST SUCCESSFUL INTERNET COMPANY IS BASED ON TWO PILLARS OF GROWTH: THE GLOBAL SPREAD OF INTERNET-STYLE CAPITALISM AND CONFIDENCE IN THE BASIC GOODNESS OF THE PEOPLE WHO DO BUSINESS ON THE SITE. BOTH IDEAS CAME UNDER ATTACK ON SEPTEMBER 11.

Just outside Berlin are the remnants of an East German checkpoint: Drewitz-Dreilinden. For nearly 40 years, it was a stark barrier between East and West, separating two cultures on the constant brink of war. One culture was built on state control and fear. The other was based on freedom, private markets, and trust.

Today, the checkpoint has been transformed into an office park, housing the German subsidiary of eBay. Soldiers have disappeared in favor of landscaped grounds and a new address: Marketplace 1. Not everyone would choose an office with such an ominous past. Yet for eBay, arguably the most successful Internet company in the world, this location is compellingly apt.

Look at eBay's constant profusion of online auctions, and you will see more than just an ultramodern form of commerce that is fueled by the Internet—a virtual World Trade Center. You will also see an intense tug-of-war between two utterly different views of human conduct. It all comes down to a few basic questions: Can we still trust people we don't know? Will our lives be better if we open our mailboxes—even our hearts—to people far away? Or is trust a dangerously naive way to live and do business, yet another casualty of September 11?

Whether by accident or by design, eBay has become a remarkable testing ground for this debate. Some 34 million people now participate in eBay, which consists of buyers and sellers from all over the world. Hardly any of them know one another. Nonetheless, they ring up commerce at a staggering rate of nearly $10 billion a year, taking it on faith that someone really will send the money or ship the goods on time.

In the overwhelming majority of cases, that trust is richly repaid. Trading partners who find each other online go on to enjoy a smooth exchange, some kind words, and maybe even a new friendship. The exceptions to eBay's culture of trust are rare but horribly disquieting. Over the years, people have accessed eBay not just to deal in Monet prints and teddy bears, but also to offer Nazi pamphlets, gruesome pornography, and mementos of convicted killers. The same technology that empowers millions of people's healthy passions also provides opportunities for much darker impulses. And the Internet makes it possible for any operator—good or bad—to affect more people's lives faster than ever before.

Even in calm times, the trade-offs are perplexing. Trust too much, and you are easy prey. Trust nobody, and you live a morose, empty life. Until September 11, most people thought that they could strike the right balance. But when a handful of airplane passengers turned out to be murderous hijackers, everyone's inner gyroscope was sent reeling. Suddenly, it was clear: We had entered a world in which some very powerful people abhor the rise of American-style capitalism—and oppose modernity itself. Whom can we trust now?

THE KINDNESS OF STRANGERS

In this altered world, some of the gutsiest and most unexpected reassessments are taking place at eBay. Now that terrorism looms larger than ever, it would be easy to let suspicion take command of our lives. But at eBay's offices and in its vast user community, people have made exactly the opposite decision. After an agonizing first few days in September, they redoubled their bet on trust

"At first, everyone at eBay was just plain stunned," says Meg Whitman, the company's president and CEO. "These attacks strike at the core of a lot of things that people believe in."

On September 11, eBay's new listings plunged 25%. As news of the terrorist strikes spread, nobody wanted to put up merchandise for sale, let alone bid on it. The eBay message boards became grieving boards. "There was such a sense of powerlessness," eBay's chief financial officer, Rajiv Dutta, recalls. Yes, eBay employees began putting flag decals by their desks and Statue of Liberty screen savers on their computers. But such gestures couldn't change anything.

Overnight, eBay's sweet-natured philosophy—articulated by the company's founder, French-Iranian immigrant Pierre Omidyar—started to seem like a painfully innocent relic of a different era. "We believe that people are basically good," eBay had declared in 1998, when it first posted its code of values on an obscure corner of its Web site. "We believe that everyone has something to contribute."

But were those thoughts really so naive? "We do $2.25 billion worth of gross sales a quarter entirely on trust," Dutta says. "The number of positive experiences that users have is staggering. This company could not work if people were so distrustful of each other."

And so, by the weekend after the September 11 attack, eBay executives decided to turn part of their Web site into one of the world's biggest fund-raising drives on behalf of the victims. EBay users would be invited to auction off anything imaginable for the benefit of charities such as the September 11th Fund. All intermediaries, including eBay and Visa, would waive their fees. The program would be known as "Auction for America." Its goal, eBay COO Brian Swette declared, would be to raise $100 million in 100 days. The millions of members of the eBay community would get a chance to demonstrate the power of good over evil.

SAFE FOR ECONOMIC DEMOCRACY?

Within a few weeks of the attack, glimmers of eBay's traditional optimism had returned. Now it was tempered with a new resolve to show that an ever-growing global community could be built on trust. Already, eBay gets 14% of its business from non-U.S. subsidiaries in countries from Germany to Korea. Instead of retrenching abroad, eBay officials vowed to press on with expansion plans that will eventually include China, Hong Kong, and Taiwan.

"We've got a vision that we call 'global economic democracy,'" explained Matt Bannick, head of international operations. "Think of someone making baskets in Belize that are ultimately sold in Germany. That person may get just $1.50 a basket, if there are the usual layers of middlemen between him or her and the ultimate buyer in a shop in Hamburg. But what if the seller and buyer could find each other on eBay? Then maybe the basket maker could earn something much closer to the full $40 that the basket is worth."

Such dreams have been on Bannick's mind for more than a decade. In 1989, he was a diplomat for the State Department, and his first posting was to Germany, as the Berlin Wall was coming down. On that assignment, he rejoiced to see the openness and freedom of Western democracy triumph over communism. But even then, he brooded about what could go wrong.

Today, Bannick is one of eBay's great optimists about world harmony. He has run eBay's international business for a year, and on his business trips to Europe, he meets Italian Vespa dealers who track their eBay feedback ratings in just the same way that Barbie-doll collectors in California do. He hears stories about Belgian postcard collectors who make friends with similar hobbyists in Florida, thanks to an introduction on eBay.

"As I spend more time on the job, I realize that different parts of the world are more similar than I thought," Bannick says. "People everywhere like to trade things. They like to get good deals. They like to develop good reputations. This is a global trading community, not just an American phenomenon."

Yet elsewhere at eBay, people know that it will be a hard fight to keep the online-auction site pleasant and safe—and that the battle isn't completely won yet. In the past three years, eBay has hired its own full-time fraud investigators to root out cases where bogus sellers are cashing buyers' checks without delivering the goods. Fraud rates have dropped, but it still isn't possible to thwart every rogue operator ahead of time.

EBay has also drafted and redrafted an increasingly strict "Offensive Materials" policy. The goal: to stop people from selling Nazi memorabilia, photos of lynchings, or anything that promotes hate, violence, or racial intolerance. But for every outrage that eBay keeps off of the site, a new problem area surfaces every month or two.

Old-timers may find such interventions jarring. When eBay was founded in 1995, it had a thoroughly libertarian bent. "If something was legal for sale," Whitman recalls, "it was legal on eBay." The company's founders and early employees took pride in not limiting what buyers and sellers could do. There was a presumption that the eBay user community would steer the company in the right direction.

That might have been appropriate four years ago, when eBay's user community was tiny. But as eBay's community surpassed the size of New York City, Whitman realized that the company's responsibilities had changed. By the end of 1998, for example, eBay had become a meaningful outpost in the firearms trade, with hundreds of weapons for sale. Buyer scrutiny was minimal. But at a meeting in January 1999, Whitman and eBay board member Howard Schultz (who is also the chairman of Starbucks) led the push to get guns off of the site. "Having them up there just wasn't appropriate," Whitman says. "It didn't fit in with the kind of company we wanted to be."

In the spring of 1999, Columbine High School in Littleton, Colorado was racked by more than a dozen deaths as two students opened fire on classmates. None of the firearms involved had come from eBay. But as the implications of that event sunk in, eBay became ever stricter about what it would sell.

Firecrackers and police badges were banned. Tobacco products were declared off-limits, and wine sales were severely restricted. And new software, which would automatically search for sale listings that included keywords associated with "hate commerce," was released. Those listings would then be purged from the site, and a customer-service specialist would review them to see if there was any reason to allow such a listing.

Even after September 11, painfully unwelcome listings popped up on eBay. Within hours after the collapse of the twin towers at the World Trade Center, a few people began offering building shards for sale. It didn't take eBay long to decide that such listings would be banned from the site "out of consideration for the many victims of this tragedy."

BIGGER. STRONGER. BETTER.

There wasn't nearly as neat a remedy for the flare- up of cynicism and suspicion that surfaced among some users following the terrorist attacks. In the everyday debate on eBay's message boards, some active sellers grumbled that the Auction for America initiative might siphon away customers and hurt their business. Others carped that people participating in the charity auction might just be looking for ways to boost their feedback rating.

Such low-level grumbling may just be part of a democracy, suggests Jim Griffith, eBay's longtime customer-service ambassador. "It isn't realistic to expect everyone in a community to agree on everything," he says. "We have our disagreements, and then we move forward."

Yet for the most part, eBay officials believe that their global community will emerge from the September 11 tragedy bigger and stronger than before. One of the most striking surprises in this area came in late September, when CFO Rajiv Dutta began advising major shareholders about the Auction for America initiative. One of his first calls was to the Janus mutual-fund company in Denver, which owns millions of eBay shares. For about 10 minutes, Dutta briefed a cluster of Janus analysts and portfolio managers about the program as they listened on a speakerphone. He explained that eBay would be foregoing significant fee revenue to make the charity auction happen, but that he and other top executives believed that it was the right thing to do.

When Dutta was done, he "didn't hear anything for five or six seconds," he recalls. "I wondered, Did I say something wrong? Do they think that this is just a big mistake?" Then Blaine Rollins, head of the flagship Janus Fund, weighed in. "Rajiv," he said, "we are so proud of what you're doing. Let us know how we can help."

Senior editor George Anders (ganders@fastcompany.com) runs *Fast Company*'s Silicon Valley bureau.

THE VALUE OF GOOD WORKS

On September 17, eBay's Auction for America made its debut at a New York news conference, where Mayor Rudolph Giuliani and Governor George Pataki joined eBay CEO Meg Whitman. Within days, members of the eBay community were selling thousands of items in the charity drive, ranging from Vietnam War medals to dinosaur teeth. "Many of us were trying to find ways to help," a Canadian seller explained. "I congratulate eBay for creating one."

Auction for America became a rallying point for other leaders who wanted to help repair America's wounds. The NFL said that it would sell memorabilia through the eBay program. So did Utah governor Mike Leavitt and Texas congresswoman Kay Granger. Jay Leno volunteered to sell one of his Harleys over the site.

Buyers in Auction for America found their spirits lifted too. More than 100 people bought drawings by Amber Moydell, an 8-year-old girl in Texas. She depicted people of all races holding hands around a simply drawn version of the globe. Among the buyers was a New York woman who wrote to the Moydell family immediately after seeing Amber's drawings.

"She said that she had lost several friends in the September 11 attack," Amber's mother, Michael Moydell, recalls. "Every time she felt that life was getting really hard, she said that she would look at Amber's drawing and take it as a reminder that there are warmhearted people out there."

BY ALAN M. WEBBER — FROM *FAST COMPANY* ISSUE 58, PAGE 130

Are All Consultants Corrupt?

THAT'S ONE POSSIBLE CONCLUSION IN THE WAKE OF THE ENRON SCANDAL. ACCORDING TO DAVID MAISTER, WHO'S BEEN STUDYING PROFESSIONAL-SERVICES FIRMS FOR MORE THAN TWENTY YEARS, IT'S TIME TO CLEAR THE AIR.

Enron's monumental bankruptcy, Global Crossing's questionable accounting practices, and Wall Street's complicity - if there is a common thread in the scandals of the day, it is the central role played by the nation's elite professional-services firms. McKinsey & Co., the bluest of blue-chip consulting firms, gave Enron its strategy—and even its former CEO. Jeffrey Skilling's model for Enron was to pattern it after a professional-services firm, to elevate the company above the lesser status of an energy company to the more rarified air of a knowledge-based, asset-light company. Andersen, among the most respected accounting firms, vouched for Enron's books. Enron was chock-full of MBAs and refugees from accounting and consulting firms. A few column inches away from Enron is Global Crossing and its founder and chairman, Gary Winnick, who is an alumnus of Drexel Burnham Lambert. The fingerprints of Wall Street's elite firms appear on some of the questionable transactions that are now under congressional scrutiny. And the world of professional-services firms—a world to which most high-flying MBAs readily aspire—is suddenly under intense review.

In that world, David Maister is the recognized expert. For more than 20 years, he has been studying professional-services firms. He has written about them, spoken to them, and consulted for them. A native of Great Britain, Maister holds degrees from the University of Birmingham, the London School of Economics, and the Harvard Business School. He taught at HBS for seven years before striking out on his own. His books (all published by the Free Press) include Managing the Professional Services Firm (1993), The Trusted Advisor (2000), Practice What You Preach: What Managers Must Do to Create a High-Achievement Culture (2001), and, most recently, First Among Equals (2002).

Fast Company sat down with Maister in his home in Boston to gain insight into the state of professional-services firms, their role in the current scandals, and the right way to be a professional.

What's your take on the business scandals that we're seeing today?

The car wreck that we're reading about in the newspapers was inevitable. It was going to happen, because professional-services firms don't practice what they preach. They're filled with smart people who understand what they should do to win. Those people talk about having a strategy with a longer-term view, but the operational reality is vastly different. They want the money right now. In practice, cash is everything.

That's how most professional-services firms operate. But are there fabulous accountants, lawyers, consultants, and investment bankers who do it right? Absolutely. What's missing are whole firms that are built on discipline and strategy. With one or two exceptions, cash is everything for a firm. It's also important to mention that the current scandals are not that special. They're special in size, but not in nature.

Is the problem with professional services due to a lapse in ethics?

The real problem is that people do what they're told. They're simply in compliance mode. What's even more interesting is that there's so much going on that's stupid. People are making the wrong calls on stuff that doesn't even come close to ethics. But that's just common practice. It's what happens inside firms, because that's how people have been raised in business. Before they even get to an ethical issue, they've been taught that if there's cash to be made, then make it. So it's not as if they were wonderful to begin with and then suddenly there was an ethical challenge and they lost their way. The message has always been that nothing trades off against cash.

Too many professional-services firms have never met a dollar they didn't like. The question that they need to ask themselves is, Do we believe in our own strategy and our own standards, even when we're tempted by cash? Good business is about having the guts to stick to a strategy. You can count on the fingers of a single maimed hand the number of professional-services firms that have the courage to stick to their strategy.

So what's wrong with the professional-services firms of today?

The problem is that they've been taught to act like businesses. But they've learned all the worst lessons of business and missed all the best ones. Tom Peters used to tell the story of McDonald's founder Ray Kroc. Someone asked Kroc what his secret of success was, and he answered, You have to be able to see the beauty in a hamburger bun. You might laugh at first, but when you think about it, that's got to be right.

What most professional-services firms don't understand is that to make the most money, you actually have to believe in the product or service that you offer and care for the customers or clients whom you serve. That isn't a religious argument; it's a business lesson. You can't dominate an industry unless you care passionately about what you do and the people you do it for.

Why don't these firms change?

Why don't they change? Let me give you an analogy from my own life. I am a fat smoker. I don't need another speech to tell me that I should stop smoking and lose weight. Clear lungs, a longer life, a better sex life—I accept that it's a fabulous strategy. But please, no more speeches. Now, people in professional services have heard all the speeches before too: Give great customer service, be a team player, manage your people. It's not that they don't believe the strategy.

The problem is, whether it's me giving up smoking or them starting to give great customer service, any kind of improvement requires short-term sacrifice and short-term pain in the name of a better long-term future. There are very few businesses that are truly interested in maximizing their future income stream.

Professional-services firms need to have an ideology. They need to know what they stand for. They need to have nonnegotiable, minimum standards. They need to be able to say, We will not accept work that goes against our standards, because that's not who we are. The problem in professional services is that because the environment is so bountiful, you can get everything wrong and still have a nice income.

I'm not picking on any one profession. They're all equally bad. They treat people poorly. They don't train well. They have no quality assurance. They don't collaborate with one another. They don't show any interest in their clients. You would think that this would kill them. But they're only competing against each other. So as long as nobody wakes up, they can all make money doing this shit. Why are there so many bad professional-services firms out there? For the same reason that there are so many fat smokers.

But don't most firms know that they're not measuring up?

Here's a little quiz that I've been giving professional-services audiences for the past seven years. First I give them three categories to classify how they feel about their work. Category one is, "I love this stuff! I just love doing it." Category two is, "I can tolerate it, but that's why they call it work. I do my job, but I have no emotional investment in it." Category three is, "How the hell did I end up doing this junk?"

The results are always the same in all professions around the world. You get about 20% who say, "I love this work"; 60% to 70% who say, "I can tolerate it"; and 10% to 20% who say that what they do is junk.

Then I give them a second question. I say, "You've told me about your work. Now tell me how you feel about your clients." Again, I give them three categories to classify how they feel. Category one is, "I really like these people. I enjoy serving them." Category two is, "I can tolerate them. I'm responsible and I give good service, but there is no real difference between today's client and tomorrow's client." Category three is, "These people are idiots who work in a boring industry."

The results for the second question are pretty much the same as for the first. About 20% love their customers, 60% to 70% can tolerate them, and 10% to 20% can't stand them.

What the numbers say is that most professionals like their jobs one day a week or less, and the rest of the time, they just tolerate what they do. Then I ask them, "Do you think your clients can tell?" To which everybody says, "Yes!" Well, what are the business implications of that? For most professional-services firms, the answer lies in their mission statement: We won't screw up, but we're nothing special.

I tell them, If that were me, I'd slit my wrists! That's true for one very simple reason: I don't want my tombstone to read, "He did tolerable stuff for tolerable people because they paid him." I'm not that much of a whore. Do I do it occasionally? Sure. I'm no more noble than anyone else. But that's not the issue. The issue is, Is that your life? Why would you want to spend your life doing stuff that you can just tolerate, working for people you don't like? Especially when you realize that you can make more money doing work that engages your passions. The only sensible business rule is, Life is too short to work for idiots. So if you're working with people who are shady or crooked, get out!

Alan M. Webber (awebber@fastcompany.com) is a *Fast Company* founding editor. Visit David Maister on the Web (http://www.davidmaister.com).

BY ALAN M. WEBBER   FROM *FAST COMPANY* JUNE 2001

New Rules: Why Values Beat Value

WHAT DO YOUR CUSTOMERS REALLY WANT? IN AN INTERVIEW, RYAN MATHEWS, COAUTHOR OF THE FORTHCOMING BOOK "THE MYTH OF EXCELLENCE," OFFERS SOME SURPRISING ANSWERS. FORGET THE LOWEST PRICE OR THE BIGGEST DISCOUNT. SHOW A LITTLE RESPECT—AND TELL THE TRUTH.

Ryan Mathews is one of those rare individuals who, if he didn't already exist, we would need to invent him.

Consider his "career" track: He got his undergraduate degree in Mongolian history and did his graduate work in philosophy. As a trained philosopher, Mathews next put his degree to work tending bar for two years at an inner-city bar in Detroit. During that same period, he was also working as a fine artist, developing his eye as a painter. Next, he migrated to writing, tackling "gonzo feature writing" for the Detroit Free Press. From there, it was a short jump to a stint as a medical writer. Then, in pursuit of a more stable salary, Mathews moved on to publishing, working as a production manager and art director for a small publishing company.

In the course of setting type for one of the magazines, Mathews discovered that he could write better than the reporters. So in addition to his design and production responsibilities, he assumed the job of copy editor and rewrite man—without telling anyone. That led to Mathews's next self-reinvention: a series of publishing posts, always moving up in responsibility and performance, which led to a remarkable run as editor of Progressive Grocer magazine, one of the most highly regarded trade magazines in the United States.

Then, three years ago, Mathews adopted his most recent intellectual identity: futurist. Joining Watts Wacker's firm, FirstMatter LLC, Mathews arrived at a job that—for the first time—integrates all of the varied roles he's played for the past 30 years: historian, philosopher, listener, reporter, artist, experience-crafter, speaker, performer, consumer-products and retailing expert.

And now add to that résumé coauthor of a smart, insightful, entertaining, and useful book about companies, customers, and the art of competition. With Fred Crawford, Mathews has written *The Myth of Excellence: Why Great Companies Never Try to Be the Best at Everything* (Crown Business, July 2001). Not unlike Mathews himself, the book is a delightful, winning combination: part strategic-analysis model, part charming storytelling, part philosophical treatise. All together, it is a great read and a focused contribution for business leaders who want to analyze their own approach to customers—and learn how to reconfigure their businesses into much more customer-centric operations.

Fast Company spoke with Ryan Mathews to get a quick fix on The Myth of Excellence. Here's what he had to say.

Your book starts with an essay that's a surprising social commentary—one that puts business into a very different light from simply offering goods and services for people to buy. In a way, you're offering the context for your view of business. What's the background? What's changed?

It used to be that what customers wanted from businesses could be described as "feature and function advocacy." In other words, customers wanted things that worked well—or at least reasonably well—and they wanted things that worked as advertised. Businesses, for their part, made things that worked reasonably well, and they expected customers to give them money. It was a transactional world. You brought your goods or services to market; I paid you for those goods or services; I went away reasonably happy with what I'd purchased; you went away reasonably happy with my money.

Now, that world worked because of some things that are different from today's world. First, there were genuine efficacy differences—that is, there was a time when Tide actually did clean clothes better than its competitors. There were Craftsman tools that came with a lifetime guarantee—and that was a superior offer. The same kinds of difference held true for appliances, cars, clothing, and furniture.

Second, as people lived their lives—not as consumers, but just as people—they had lots of sources of institutional reinforcement. Authority figures were generally regarded as good guys. Schools worked. Leaders were leaders; people played by the rules. People's emotional, psychological, and social values were reinforced by all kinds of supporting institutions.

Fast forward a few years, and what happens? You've got the general dislocation created by rapid technological change. In mature industries, you've got the closing of the efficacy gap. Tide may still get your clothes cleaner than any other laundry powder, but you'd need an electron microscope to detect it—and most people don't have an electron microscope in their laundry room. In general, tools don't break, so the Craftsman guarantee isn't as important. Cars, more or less, have the same degree of quality—or lack of quality, depending on your point of view. And then there's the decline of leadership, a collective failure of the institutions that reinforced people's values.

So what's the punch line? What is the consequence?

All of this had an unexpected and interesting result: People have turned to commerce to reinforce their personal values. And that hasn't happened before.

You were writing a book on customers—defining five attributes of companies' offerings and three levels for each attribute. And, instead, you discovered a totally different kind of relationship between companies and customers. How did you reach such an unexpected insight?

We came to this conclusion in a very roundabout way. Between the two of us, Fred and I have about 40 years of experience studying consumer behavior. We designed a very simple 5,000-person survey, asking people about price, product, access, service, and experience. Before we even sent it out, we knew what the answers were going to be. And then the answers came back, and Fred and I were amazed that 5,000 consumers could get of follow-up interviews to figure out why people couldn't give us the right answers. We found that what we thought were simple questions had impossible answers. No one could get them straight. The whole pattern of answers was the reverse of what we thought they should have been.

Those results made us go back and redrill through our research. When we did that, we got a commercial version of Alice in Wonderland. When we gave people a choice, they said things that we'd never seen before. Words like discount, sale, and price didn't show up at all. But value-proposition words—respect, trust, sincerity—showed up with incredible strength.

Here's the headline that goes at the top of that story: It turns out that it's the values, not the value. It's not just the value that you're offering the customer; it's the values of the store, reflected in the way the store does business. What people told us was, "We want to do business with people who are fair and honest. We want to do business with people who respect us as individuals. Don't give us phony discounts. Don't give us a fake smile. Don't have a greeter at the door who's there like a zombie, pretending to welcome us, but who's really checking for shoplifters."

The message from consumers is this: In a world where people think that the government is corrupt, that the church is corrupt, that the schools are corrupt, show us a business that isn't corrupt, and we'll do business with you for life.

After I read your book, what do I do Monday morning to do a better job of customer relevancy?

Peter Drucker once said that if you were a world-beater, in most businesses you'd probably have about 30% of the market—and 30% of the market would make you a killer success story.

And Peter Drucker's next line, of course, is that 7 out of 10 people aren't doing business with you. You need to go talk to those 7 people—in a way, they're more important than the 3 who are doing business with you. You also need to deal with alignment issues: You need to find out what store, what airline, what business your employees are patronizing, your managers are patronizing, your vendors are working with. And you should analyze your direct competitors—go talk to their customers too. Then you not only know who your customers think you are, you also know what your competitors' customers think they are.

You can see whether your offerings are in alignment with what the market really is responding to. Most companies aren't in alignment. Most companies aren't running businesses for their customers; they're running businesses for themselves.

Alan Webber (awebber@fastcompany.com) is a founding editor of *Fast Company*. Contact Ryan Mathews (ryan.mathews@firstmatter.com) by email.

DISCUSSION QUESTIONS FOR SECTION 1

1. How did eBay attempt to build trust after September 11, 2001?
2. What would your response be to the title of the second article: Are all consultants corrupt? Agree or disagree? Defend your answer with two reasons.
3. What are the "new rules" that should govern business' interaction with customers?

THE ENRON DEBACLE

This section discusses the demise of the seventh largest corporation in the United States in the year 2001. The Enron unraveling was a watershed event for American business. Prior to Enron's bankruptcy, the financial markets and investors felt that growth and diversification into vastly different markets was generally a good thing. As the events unfolded, it became clear that much of Enron's growth was fueled by Special Purpose Entities, which allowed Enron to "hide" much of its debt. The media, and not just the business press, reported extensively on Enron in late 2001 and throughout 2002. In fact, prosecutors and the media seemed to be inspired by the Enron saga and were much more vigilant in examining the scandals at other corporations. Consequently, companies such as Global Crossing, Tyco, WorldCom, and Martha Stewart (the person and the brand) were investigated for a number of questionable financial practices.

This section contains four articles. The first deals with Enron employees. *Fast Company* is one of the few outlets that reported in any depth on middle- and lower-level Enron employees. The first article tells a fascinating story of some of the several different individuals who worked at Enron. The reader may be surprised to learn what these employees, who in most cases lost their jobs, had to say about their experiences at Enron. The initiative of Rebekah Rushing, who actually took action to help fellow laid-off Enron colleagues, is a heart-warming story.

The second selection deals with Wall Street and argues that "the Street" did not play by ethical rules prior to the Enron bankruptcy. The issue of legality versus unethical action is discussed in-depth in this article. To this author, the most important theme is the culture of dishonesty on Wall Street. In the later months of 2002, some Wall Street CEO's were endeavoring to change the culture at these firms to one that is more ethically driven.

The third article provides six lessons on how one might spot another Enron scandal in the future. These lessons include closer scrutiny of financial statements and accounting practices (some of which are now illegal under the Sarbanes-Oxley Act) and interacting directly with customers as indicators of how the company is doing. The last lesson pertains to an examination of CEOs and their handling of criticism. A particularly troubling aspect of Enron and most of the other business scandals of the early 21st century is that CEOs and top management were the ones engaging in unethical behavior.

The final selection in this section examines the world after Enron. This article speaks more directly to business executives than to students. However, the author provides some excellent advice in his five points pertaining to the post-Enron environment. Some of the pitfalls this author addresses are complacency, not consulting experts, only planning for expected consequences, and believing the world is not complex and the future can be predicted. The article should serve as a guide to student readers, who might use it later in their career when confronted with ethical dilemmas. Insights are presented as to how companies can be better managed from both an ethical and operational standpoint.

BY CHARLES FISHMAN   FROM *FAST COMPANY* ISSUE 58, PAGE 102

What If You'd Worked at Enron?

WE'VE ALL HEARD THE SAME ENRON STORY: EXECUTIVES AT THE TOP BEHAVING BADLY, VICTIMS AT THE BOTTOM LOSING THEIR SAVINGS. BUT THE TRUTH IS IN THE MIDDLE.

It wasn't just that working at Enron was hectic, or demanding, or urgent. What made working at Enron different was that it was intoxicating. It took otherwise unglamorous work—scheduling natural-gas pipelines, developing electricity pricing models, managing a fiber-optic network—and gave it a powerful sense of mission.

Phyllis Anzalone was the first person Enron dispatched to California in 1996 to sell electricity as a retail commodity. The opportunity, she says, "lit me on fire. It was like a drug."

Helena Payne worked for 24 years at Enron and its predecessor, Houston Natural Gas. She liked the company so much that she recruited her daughter Rebekah Rushing to work there. Rushing, an administrative assistant, adopted the work ethic of an executive. Last summer, she took her laptop on her family vacation to Lake Tahoe, and she worked three of the five days she was there.

Charles Weiss left a 19-year career at Sprint to join Enron in March 2001—for a job that lasted just 9 months. "The risk," Weiss says, "was not going to Enron and not having the chance to fulfill my aspirations."

Steve Kromer worked for 10 years to become an energy-conservation expert before he joined Enron. "For an energy-efficiency nut," says Kromer, "Enron was nirvana."

But even as Enron inspired these employees, there were things about the company that didn't add up.

Helena Payne reviewed and reimbursed Enron corporate expense accounts. For years, she and her fellow "accounting ladies" found themselves authorizing reimbursement for employees who they were sure had paid for prostitutes.

And Steve Kromer always had the sense that for his boss's bosses, "If the idea was great enough, it didn't matter whether you ever actually did it. It was more like, 'Let's book $3 trillion in revenue and move on.'"

During Enron's unraveling, the largest corporate bankruptcy in U.S. history, most attention has been focused on two places: the deception, greed, and malfeasance at the top and the financial victims at the bottom.

But life at Enron, as at most companies, was lived in the middle. Not too far from the top, not too far from the bottom, a battalion of familiar white-collar employees worked every day, their lives consumed, brightened, then betrayed by Enron.

What follows are snapshots of the worlds of five ex-Enroners, people who can explain, how did the company inspire such passion? People willing to answer the question, were there any hints of the problems that brought Enron down? And people who can help us answer the single most important question of all: What would you have done if you had worked at Enron?

PHYLLIS ANZALONE: THE TRUE BELIEVER

How badly did Phyllis Anzalone want to work for Enron? In January 1996, at the start of energy deregulation, she interviewed with two Enron executives and issued an ultimatum: "I said, 'You can either hire me or compete against me.'"

What did working at Enron do for Anzalone? For one thing, it made her a lot of money, so much that the company's failure cost her about $1 million. More important, it made her. It took her from being a reasonably successful facilities-management salesperson from rural Louisiana and propelled her into the ranks of sales superstars. It changed her view of herself; it confirmed what she thought she could achieve. "Enron had a profound effect on my life," she says. "As devastating as it was, I'm glad I did it. It was like being on steroids every day."

And what does Anzalone think of the executives who ran Enron—and then ran it into the ground? "They are scum," she says. "They are crooks, and they are traitors. They betrayed many people's trust, including mine. Jeff Skilling is lying. Every single employee at Enron knows he's lying."

All of which makes Anzalone a true believer. "Working for Enron was a commitment," she says. "I worked my ass off."

Four months after Enron hired her, Anzalone went to San Francisco to crack California's retail-electricity market. She was an "originator"—she "originated," or sold, energy-supply contracts. "I concentrated on Silicon Valley and health care. Those were critical operating environments that used a lot of energy," Anzalone says. "My goal was to show businesses how they could improve on the 'do nothing' position. That was our biggest competitor—companies who decided to do nothing, to just keep getting electricity from the utility."

Eventually, she had Applied Materials, Sutter Health, and all of Kaiser Permanente's sprawling California facilities among her customers. "It was a brand-new industry doing things that had never been done before. It was the most fun I've ever had."

Anzalone was offering customers a seemingly simple proposition: a fixed rate for electricity, going out two, five, even six years, priced 5% below regulated rates. In fact, the sales were extremely complex. The price was based on consumption in 15-minute increments. The contracts were 3 inches thick. "No one understood those contracts," says Anzalone, "not even me."

Enron Energy Services (EES), Anzalone says, "was an entrepreneurial culture. If you met your goals, you could double your salary. I was always doubling my goals—or more. In the first five months of 2001, I quadrupled my goals." In 2000 and 2001, she earned an annual salary well into six figures.

That was the part of Enron that Anzalone thrived on. Then there was the part of Enron that she shunned: the culture of Enron's Houston headquarters. She disliked it so much that she managed to avoid being stationed there for four of her five years at the company. "I wanted to produce and be left alone," she says. "I didn't like the politics of Houston."

The problem was that Anzalone didn't fit the Enron pedigree. Much of her appeal is her high-energy, up-by-the-bootstraps hustle. Much of Enron's cachet was built on its ability to attract the polished graduates of the nation's leading business schools. "The arrogance of the leadership always offended me," she says. "I always had a great boss at EES. But I always said, 'I like the people I work with. I hate the people I work for.'"

Nor was Anzalone comfortable with Enron's free-spending ways, even when she benefited from them. "The company never did pay much attention to expenses, and it always bothered me," she says. In April 2001, EES sent its top 75 performers and their spouses to the Four Seasons Resort Nevis, in the West Indies, for four all-expenses-paid days. "The last day we were there," says Anzalone, "they flew in the Fabulous Thunderbirds for two hours of dancing. They flew the band to Nevis." The trip cost $1.2 million—$16,000 a couple.

More than anything, because she believed so deeply in Enron, Anzalone feels deeply betrayed. "Emotionally," she says, "I'll feel a sense of loss for a long time. I'm incredibly disappointed in senior management. They lied to the shareholders, they lied to the employees, and they lied to the people at Enron who were making things happen." She pauses. "You know, if you were at Enron, you loved it."

HELENA PAYNE: THE GOOD SOLDIER, REBEKAH RUSHING: THE GOOD ASSISTANT

Helena Payne is a small woman, reserved and watchful, the kind of woman who seems to know more than she feels the need to say. What she says about Enron and its predecessor, Houston Natural Gas, comes from working there for 24 years. "The backbone of Enron was the good people," Payne says, "not the people you're hearing about in the news." Because of the damage Enron's bankruptcy has done to her retirement savings, her husband will probably have to keep working. "I feel hurt," she says, "but I don't feel hate. Anger doesn't do anything but give you bad health."

Payne spent her career in accounts payable, much of that time reviewing employee expense accounts. "I really liked doing the expense reports," she says. "I met really nice people from all over the company. And I got to do the traveling they did without leaving my desk."

Payne handled expenses for the whole company, from front-line workers to high-level executives. It was a quiet, revealing vantage from which to observe Enron's way of doing business. What Payne saw was a cascade of extravagances. "Mostly it was entertainment," she says. "Lots of entertainment. They'd take hundreds of people to a concert. We always thought, That's a lot more money than should be spent on company business."

And then there were the expenses from strip clubs. The "accounting ladies," says Payne, "kept questioning some of the places we were getting charges for, striptease places. We knew they were prostitution-type places. We paid for prostitutes. The money those people were being reimbursed for, it was a whole lot more than dinner and a couple of drinks. Thousands of dollars. They explained that this was their procedure to entertain their customers, to get more business for the company. That's the way they put it to us."

After complaining for years, the accounting clerks were eventually given a list of adult-entertainment venues that they weren't supposed to reimburse for. "They started telling us, Things have changed," says Payne. "They gave us a list of names that we weren't supposed to pay for. When you see those places, they said, a red light should go off in your head."

When Enron collapsed, Payne lost nearly 80% of her six-figure 401(k) account. But her own personal accounting of her time with Enron is more accepting than resentful. "I had faith in the company," Payne says. "I had faith in Ken Lay. You can't lose faith in people because of a bad apple. If I had the choice to do it again, I would still do the same thing."

Rebekah Rushing, like her mother, looks back on her time at Enron with few regrets. "I wish I still worked there," she says. "Everybody was go, go, go. You gave 110%." Rushing had a whirlwind seven-and-a-half-year career at Enron, during which she had five jobs. "Not a lot of places would give you the kind of opportunities Enron did without a four-year degree," she says. "I loved it."

By the end of her Enron career, Rushing had advanced to a high-level assistant position, with four assistants reporting to her. She'd get to the office around 5 AM, go to the gym for a morning workout, be at her desk by 6:45, and often stay at work until 7 PM. Last year she earned $80,000, including overtime. "If you were a good assistant at Enron," Rushing says, "you were your boss's right hand, and he relied on you. You were the quiet partner behind the scenes who got everything done." Of the senior people who have become newspaper headlines since Enron's bankruptcy, Rushing says, "I knew them all. Or, at least, I knew their assistants."

As is often the case in business, the assistants had their own network. And as is always the case with good assistants, they knew what they could—and could not—discuss. Rushing worked out with Andrew Fastow's assistant every morning at the Enron gym. "We were both single moms with teenage kids," Rushing says. "We talked about that. She was a breast-cancer survivor. We talked about that too." One thing that they didn't talk about was their bosses. "You understand why people can't talk about things," she says. "At my boss's level, there were things going on that I knew about but did not talk about. Reorganizations, restructurings. If you did talk, you didn't last very long in that kind of position."

Rushing saw some of the signs of Enron's collapse last December. "When FedEx wouldn't let us ship using the Enron account number, when they wanted a credit card, that was a bad sign," she says. "I'm thinking, a Fortune 500 company where you can't use the FedEx number? Hmmm..." Rushing is an optimist by nature, but she's also nobody's fool: She started her own job search weeks before Enron filed for bankruptcy, and she landed at Avalon Energy LLC in Houston.

But she's still using her organizational skills to stay connected to her former Enron colleagues. Just 10 days after being laid off, Rushing and two friends set up a fund at Humble Community Bank to help other ex-Enroners. She deposited $90 of her own money to get the account started. By January 18, when the Associated Press wrote a story about the fund, it had $170. The day the AP story ran, Rushing got a phone call from the bank president saying a check for $68,000 had arrived.

"I thought she was teasing me," Rushing says. "I made her fax me a copy of the check. I was in tears. I couldn't believe it." Washington politicians, seeking to cleanse their political campaigns of Enron contributions, had decided to "return" them to Enron's fired employees—through Rushing's fund. That first check for $68,000 came from New York senator Charles Schumer's campaign. Since then, nearly $290,000 has arrived. And while celebrities like Jesse Jackson and elected officials like Congresswoman Sheila Jackson Lee have talked about helping former Enron workers, Rushing and her two friends have actually done it: Their fund has paid out $280,000 to 230 ex-Enroners, paying mortgages and utility bills directly and providing "cash cards" they can use at local grocery stores.

Rushing has little thought for those who brought Enron down. "I don't like watching those guys testify on TV," she says. "I have more important things to do with my time. What goes around comes around. I don't wish bad on anybody. But whatever is supposed to happen to those men will happen."

CHARLES WEISS: THE SHORT TIMER

Charles Weiss is a torn man.

He knows that he had no choice but to leave Sprint for Enron. It was the right job, at the right moment, at the right place.

And he knows that if he had somehow resisted Enron and stayed at Sprint, he would still have a job. The guy they hired to replace him—two guys, actually—are both still working. Charles Weiss, meanwhile, is jobless in the worst telecom downturn in his 30 years in the business. "I beat myself up all the time," he says. "Then I look back, and I did what I did for all the right reasons. Who could have foreseen?"

Charles Weiss is a big man, with big hands that have seen plenty of outdoor work. His last job at Sprint had him driving around Houston in a truck, keeping Sprint's advanced fiber network and its supporting equipment operating. At 48, after 19 years with Sprint, Weiss figured he had about 15 years of work left, and he was ready to move up. But Sprint was headquartered near Kansas City, Kansas. Enron, headquartered in Houston, had just put its own 18,000-mile broadband fiber-optic network in the ground. The company wanted Weiss to be its network-capacity manager, running the equipment he already knew, but from behind a computer screen. Enron offered more money, bonuses, and stock options. Joining Enron Broadband Services (EBS) seemed like the smart move.

So in March 2001, Weiss took the leap.

His first discovery was that EBS didn't have many customers. "If you consider the capacity of the equipment they had installed," says Weiss, "they were using less than 10%. If you consider the capacity of the fiber in the ground, they were using less than 1%."

Enron had based its entire strategy on being "asset light." And here it was sitting on a very real, brand-new, $1.2 billion fiber network that was 99% dark, 99% unproductive. What to do with an expensive, fast-depreciating hard asset that can't generate revenue? Turn it into a financial asset. Or, at least, try.

Weiss got swept into the world of commodities trading. He spent a lot of time supporting the broadband trading desk. "My job was to make sure that we could actually provide the capacity and equipment that we were promising," says Weiss.

The problem was that Enron's way of doing business didn't add up. "They would sometimes trade part of their network for capacity on someone else's lines between, say, New York and Washington, DC," says Weiss. "Normally, you only do that if you have a customer. But they didn't have any customers. They never planned to use that capacity between New York and DC to send signals—they were just doing it to make the books look better. Did I think it was odd? Yes and no. It was odd. But it could be an effective way of doing business if the equipment is just sitting there anyway. The problem is, they did the deal just to do the deal. Not because it made real business sense."

Weiss was an Enron short timer. But in just nine months, he had a complete, compressed Enron career. He worked for five different bosses. He put in 12- and 14-hour days. He "found" and accounted for about $40 million in network equipment that the company seemed not to know that it owned. And then he was abruptly let go.

Which explains why Charles Weiss is a torn man. When he looks back, he concludes that the real risk would have been to stay at his job at Sprint. "The risk was not going to Enron and not having the chance to fulfill my aspirations," he says.

But sometimes, when he lets himself, Weiss thinks about the people who ran Enron, and then he gets angry. "They make me sick," he says. "They deceived everybody." Weiss remembers a day last May when then-CEO Jeffrey Skilling came down to the Enron tower's 44th floor, where broadband was based, to talk to employees. "He told us that the broadband division by itself was worth $50 a share in stockholder value," says Weiss.

STEVE KROMER: THE CONVERT

When Steve Kromer, now 42, went to work at Enron in early 2000, he had to buy all new clothes. The shorts and T-shirts that had suited him for 10 years as an energy-conservation expert at Lawrence Berkeley National Laboratory weren't going to cut it at Enron.

"I pulled back to, like, the school pictures of me when I was 5 years old, when my mother used to dress me up," says Kromer, laughing. "Classic, fit-in kind of clothes." Enron, he knew, was a place "where you can't afford to be a wild-ass hippie."

But for Kromer, the new clothes were a disguise. With almost 20 years invested in energy-conservation work in nonprofits and research labs, Kromer went to Enron with his own agenda. He wanted to use the energy, creativity, and drive of Enron to transform energy conservation from a feel-good proposition to a financially compelling business. "Conservation wouldn't be greener-than-thou, and it wouldn't be holier-than-thou," says Kromer. "It would just be good, clean solutions."

But a funny thing happened to Steve Kromer along the way. More than his clothes changed. The guy who loves the cool, clean air of Berkeley, California discovered a new part of himself in Enron's 50-story silver tower cutting into Houston's muggy haze. "Before I went to Enron, business had a bad connotation, really," says Kromer. "That's still the old hippie in me. But I discovered that good business is as exciting as good science."

Although energy conservation might seem an odd business for the world's largest energy conglomerate, the group Kromer joined was classic Enron. The idea was for conservation to become a full partner in the energy market, alongside the generation and buying of power. For Enron, where everything was fungible, conservation made financial sense: The company could help its customers save energy, then resell those savings to someone else. For customers, the deal was this: Enron would assess how much energy could be saved over, say, 10 years, and what equipment retrofits were necessary, then pay customers part of the savings up front, as well as a fee to grant Enron the right to do the conservation project. Enron and the customer would split any additional savings. And, once the conservation projects were done, Enron would, of course, bundle the contracts for resale to investors.

What was so great about Enron's approach, says Kromer, was that the company "didn't give a shit about energy efficiency. It was just about the money to them."

Kromer's expertise—evaluating and measuring how much energy was being saved in a particular setting—fit Enron quite well. He took classes at Enron in financial derivatives. He taught his field engineers to think about risk assessment and probabilities. He learned to speak Enron's language of marginal rates, proper incentivization, and commodity price curves. He began to think about conservation and engineering in a whole new light. "With conservation, you have to become risk managers, not just engineers," Kromer says. "That's what Enron was all about—risk-adjusted engineering."

The greatest challenge was the competition within Enron. "The internal politics were real cutthroat," says Kromer. "You had to fight for what you believed in, so you'd fight, you'd get beat up, you'd get depressed. And then the next day you would win—and you'd be on top of the world again."

Kromer sometimes felt naive about business. But when his bosses at Enron used phrases like "earnings management," it made him uncomfortable. "I thought, If everybody gets this, well, that's obviously the 'adult' way of doing business," Kromer says. "But I always had the sense that if the idea was great enough, it didn't matter whether you ever actually did it. There wasn't a lot of patience at Enron for the time it would take to get those applications in the ground. It was more like, 'Let's book $3 trillion in revenue and move on.'"

In the end, Kromer says, the energy asset-management group "saved something like the total energy consumption of Rhode Island. Well, maybe not quite that much." And it produced for Kromer not just a new way of thinking about conservation, but a new way of thinking about himself. "I came out a whole different person," he says. "I was crazy to begin with, but now I've seen a whole new world of possibilities."

The vision of conservation as a full partner in the world of energy is something Kromer is trying to take beyond Enron. He hopes that that creative part of the Enron legacy isn't totally lost in the anger over the scandal. "Enron was a passionate place. I hope people remember it for what it could have been too."

Charles Fishman (cnfish@mindspring.com), a *Fast Company* senior editor, wrote most recently about Biogen.

BY JOHN ELLIS   FROM *FAST COMPANY* ISSUE 58, PAGE 116

Wall Street's Den of Thieves

IF YOU FOLLOW THE TRAIL OF DECEIT FROM ENRON TO ITS NATURAL LAIR, IT ONLY LEADS TO ONE DESTINATION: WALL STREET. HERE'S WHY.

The first thing you learn on Wall Street: Earnings don't mean anything. Everyone assumes that earnings are financially engineered (sometimes downward!) to meet a variety of stakeholder expectations. The key expectation—the one that stakeholders want companies to meet—is steady growth. Earnings that spike and swoon set off alarm bells at places like Fidelity. Steady growth makes fund managers feel calm and content.

That's exactly what big companies—such as General Electric, IBM, Wal-Mart, and, for a time, Enron—deliver. Go back and read the quarterly reports of those companies over the past few years, and you'll feel as if you've taken Valium, so steady and predictable is the metronome of their results.

The second thing you learn on Wall Street has to do with the length of the auditor's letter and the number of footnotes included. Simply put, shorter and fewer is better than longer and more. If the auditor's letter is a paragraph long, go directly to the footnotes. If the auditor's letter is two paragraphs long, read the footnotes carefully. If the auditor's letter is four paragraphs long, all hands on deck and hedge your position. For the record, Enron's auditors wrote long letters that had a lot of footnotes.

The third thing you learn on Wall Street is that cash flow and sales are really what matter (since earnings can be engineered). If a company is booking revenue and its cash flow is strong, then it has flexibility. And if the company is well managed—if the people in charge know what they're doing—then it's probably worth more tomorrow than it is today. That makes it a buy if it's a stock or a bond. During the run-up years from 1996 to 2000, Enron appeared to be all that and more.

The fourth thing you learn on Wall Street—and this one is what they call a "job ender" or a "job keeper"—is that one hand washes the other. If the firm that you work for happens to do a lot of other business with a firm that you've been assigned to cover, you do not ever forget that there is no "I" in "team." You are on the team, and you will do what's right for the team. If you don't, well, don't kid yourself: No one is irreplaceable. That's why Enron was always a strong buy with all of those firms that did business with the company. Even as the stock sank like a stone during the spring, summer, and fall of 2001, ENE was always a buy or a strong buy. There's no one on Wall Street who doesn't understand that one hand washes the other.

After the music stopped and the stock tanked and Enron collapsed into bankruptcy, everyone on Wall Street pretended to be absolutely shocked that such a thing could happen. Happily enough, the more excitable members of the press and their allies in the Democratic Party saw Enron's collapse as a huge opportunity to rebrand

33

President George W. Bush and his Republican friends as the running dogs of dastardly corporate interests. Enron CEO Kenneth Lay, ex-CEO Jeffrey Skilling, and ex-CFO Andrew Fastow were all quickly sketched as Dr. Evils, and the games (known in Washington as congressional hearings) began.

The hearings, of course, have been a joke. Andersen's hapless David Duncan, former lead auditor for Enron, was the first sacrificial offering. Next up was Skilling, who declined to take the Fifth Amendment. Skilling's lack of contrition discombobulated hearing members, causing them to embark on great flights of rhetoric in which they denounced the perfidy and the heinousness of the whole affair. Next came Lay, who did take the Fifth, thus enabling various senators to slap him around at will. On and on it went, each hearing dumber and more irrelevant than the next. The net result was disgust—shared equally between Enron and the members.

Sensing that the Enron scandal was not playing out as they had hoped, the members directed their attention toward Wall Street, and a shower of subpoenas rained. Wall Street's response (figuratively speaking) was, "Go ahead. Make my day." After all, Wall Street is the mother lode of political fund-raising, and 2002 is an election year. The congressional subpoenas were fishing lines with no bait and no hook. The exercise had everything to do with headlines and nothing to do with substance.

And for good reason. Because at the core of Enron's collapse is the fact that virtually everything the company did was legal. Accounting and financial engineering obey rules—not laws, morals, or notions of right and wrong. If Andersen, Ernst & Young, and PricewaterhouseCoopers operate within the rules of accounting as outlined by the FASB and the SEC, then it doesn't matter if the company that they're auditing covers up debt, misstates earnings, or misleads investors. Tough luck. The rules were obeyed. If accounting regulations don't specifically say, "Do not create an offshore SPE collateralized by company stock to keep debt off the company's balance sheet," then all the $600-per-hour brainpower that money can buy will find a way to do it. And it will be legal.

So if Enron's actions weren't a crime, and they weren't a political scandal, then what were they? I've spent the better part of two months talking to people on Wall Street and around the country about Enron. I've read everything that I could get my hands on since the company's collapse became a scandal. Here's what I come away with: Enron was nothing more than an old Wall Street scam called the "pump and dump."

Experienced Wall Street watchers define the pump and dump as a private selling spree conducted in the middle of a public-relations blitz, which is designed to pump up the price of a stock. That was exactly what Enron's senior management did in the first quarter of 2001, hyping a target price of $120 per share while selling blocks of the company's stock by the boatload. And it appears that they did it again in July and August of last year—but this time by other means.

Concerned about a cascading stock price (and fearful that its employees would begin to bail out of its stock), Enron switched its 401(k) administrator, firing Charles Schwab and signing up UBS Warburg. Why any company would fire Charles Schwab as its 401(k) administrator is a complete mystery—unless that company wanted to freeze employee stock selling. Significantly, a freeze is required when a 401(k) shifts from one administrator to another.

The pump and dump is now the focus of the SEC's investigation into Enron. It is likely that charges will be filed soon. The government's chances of "winning" are fairly good. The chances of successful prosecution of Enron management on charges of fraud or criminal malfeasance, however, are not nearly as good, since the gray areas of private-partnership accounting, debt securitization, and all the rest of its complex business transactions are as vast as the North Sea.

But the most important thing that I learned is this: Enron is not the story. The larger, more important story is the whole culture of dishonesty on what we call Wall Street. It starts with a lie: Earnings don't mean anything; they can be engineered. It is seconded by another lie: Those financially engineered numbers are right. It is complicated by yet more lies: Sales revenue and cash flow can be manipulated as well. And then it is all locked down in a code of omerta: Enron is a strong buy!

The next Wall Street scandal will probably be called the "lazy Susan" or the "round-tripper." Lazy Susans are revenue deals that work as follows: Company A gives company B $400 million. Company B, after an insignificant amount of time, spins the $400 million back to company A. And both companies book $400 million as "revenue." It is alleged that lazy-Susan deals are endemic in the information-technology and telecom sectors and may well have spread to financial services and the media. Global Crossing, which went belly-up in January, is just one of many companies charged with spinning the wheel.

If lazy Susans turn out to be epidemic, then investors will know that on Wall Street, earnings don't mean anything, revenue doesn't mean anything, and cash flow doesn't mean anything. They will suspect that every analyst is out there to deceive— and, in some cases, to pump-and-dump on television. That's a gigantic crisis of confidence. That's what we're approaching, unless Wall Street, the SEC, and the political community get their act together. Don't hold your breath.

John Ellis (jellis@fastcompany.com) is a writer and consultant based in New York.

How to Spot the Next Enron

WANT TO KNOW HOW TO AVOID BEING FOOLED BY THE NEXT TOO-GOOD-TO-BE-TRUE STOCK-MARKET DARLING? JUST REMEMBER THESE SIX TIPS FROM THE CYNICS OF WALL STREET, THE SHORT SELLERS.

If only we could have spotted the rascals ahead of time. That's the lament of anyone who bought Enron stock a year ago, or who worked at a now-collapsed company like Global Crossing or who trusted any corporate forecast that proved way too upbeat. How could we have let ourselves be fooled? And how do we make sure that we don't get fooled again?

It's time to visit with some serious cynics. Some of the shrewdest advice comes from Wall Street's short sellers, who make money by betting that certain stocks will fall in price. They had a tough time in the 1990s, when it paid to be optimistic. But it has been their kind of year. Almost every day, new accounting jitters rock the stock market. And if you aren't asking about hidden partnerships and earnings manipulation—the sort of outrages that short sellers love to expose—you risk being blindsided by yet another business wipeout.

Think of short sellers as being akin to veteran cops who walk the streets year after year. They pick up subtle warning signs that most of us miss. They see through alibis. And they know how to quiz accomplices and witnesses to put together the whole story, detail by detail. It's nice to live in a world where we can trust everything we're told because everyone behaves perfectly. But if the glitzy addresses of Wall Street have given way to the tough sidewalks of Mean Street these days, we might as well get smart about the neighborhood.

The first rule of these streets, says David Rocker, a top New York money manager who has been an active short seller for more than two decades, is not to get mesmerized by a charismatic chief executive. "Most CEOs are ultimately salesmen," Rocker says. "If they showed up on your doorstep and said, 'I've got a great vacuum cleaner,' you wouldn't buy it right away. You'd want to see if it works. It's the same thing with a company."

A legendary case in point involves John Sculley, former CEO of Apple Computer. In 1993, he briefly became chief executive of a little wireless data company called Spectrum Information Technologies and spoke glowingly of its prospects. Spectrum's stock promptly tripled. But those who had looked closely at Spectrum's technology weren't nearly as impressed.

Just four months later, Sculley quit, saying that Spectrum's founders had misled him. The company restated its earnings, backing away from some aggressive treatment of licensing revenue that had inflated profits. The stock crashed. The only ones who came out looking smart were the short sellers who disregarded the momentary excitement of having a big-name CEO join the company. Instead, those short sellers focused on the one question that mattered: Are Spectrum's products any good?

So in the wake of Enron, you want to know what to look for in other companies. Or, more to the point, you need to know what to look for in your own company, so you're not stuck explaining what happened to your missing 401(k) fund. Here are six basic pointers from the short-selling community.

1. *Watch cash flow, not reported net income.* During Enron's heyday from 1999 to 2000, the company reported very strong net income—aided, we now know, by dubious accounting exercises. But the actual amount of cash that Enron's businesses generated wasn't nearly as impressive. That's no coincidence.

   Companies can create all sorts of adjustments to make net income look artificially strong—witness what we've seen so far with Enron and Global Crossing. But there's only one way to show strong cash flow from operations: Run the business well.

2. *Take a wary look at acquisition binges.* Some of the most spectacular financial meltdowns of recent years have involved companies that bought too much, too fast. Cendant, for example, grew fast in the mid-1990s by snapping up the likes of Days Inn, Century 21, and Avis but overreached when it bought CUC International Inc., a direct-marketing firm. Accounting irregularities at CUC led to massive write-downs in 1997, which sent the combined company's stock plummeting.

3. *Be mindful of income-accelerating tricks.* Conservative accounting says that long-term contracts should not be treated as immediate windfalls that shower all of their benefits on today's financial statements. Sell a three-year magazine subscription, and you've got predictable obligations until 2005. Those expenses will slowly flow onto your financial statements—and it's prudent to book the income gradually as well.

   But in some industries, aggressive practitioners like to put jumbo profits on the books all at once. Left for later are worries about how to deal with the eventual costs of those long-term deals. In a recent Barron's interview, long-time short seller Jim Chanos identified such "gain on sale" accounting tricks as a sure sign that the management is being too aggressive for its own good.

   Very early in his career, Chanos exposed such shenanigans at Baldwin-United, a piano maker that diversified into the insurance business. Last year, he blew the whistle on similar mischief at Enron. As Chanos pointed out, companies that adopt fast-buck accounting will find it much too tempting to "create earnings out of thin air" by entering into deals that don't make any long-term sense—but that look profitable for now.

4. *Talk to customers.* Do they really use the product? Do they like it? Are they still in business? Anyone who looks at the telecom-equipment industry could have dodged a year of stock-market disasters by noticing in late

2000 that the industry stars (Cisco, Lucent, and Nortel) were selling heavily to independent telecom companies that were teetering on the brink of insolvency. If the customers are going bust, they probably won't be buying much more from even the greatest of vendors.

5. *Watch stock sales by top company executives.* It's routine for company executives to say that their stock is undervalued and has a great future. But if they all believe that, then why do some of them hurry to unload shares at today's prices? Minor selling to pay tax bills or to finance a few of life's luxuries is one thing. But when executives unload more than $1 billion of stock over the course of a few years—as they did at Global Crossing—warning sirens should go off.

Pay extra-close attention to what the chief financial officer does. In many companies that are built on shaky foundations, the CEO, the top sales executives, and even the technological aces may stay committed to the very end. After all, who can fault them for believing their own story? But the CFO usually has the most realistic sense of what the business is really worth.

6. *See how CEOs handle criticism.* Secure bosses know that not everyone on Wall Street will like their story. They handle critics calmly. CEOs with something to hide are more likely to start shouting when someone challenges their business.

Look at what Enron's now-departed CEO, Jeffrey Skilling, did in the spring of 2001, when he was addressing Wall Street's elite during a quarterly teleconference. One analyst asked him why Enron didn't provide a balance sheet detailing its profit statements. Instead of sharing data—or even offering a civil explanation—Skilling publicly dismissed the questioner as "an asshole." Listeners were shocked at the time. Today, they regard Skilling's snide retort as an unforgettable sign of trouble.

Most of all, the short sellers say, stay vigilant. It's tempting to fall in love with a business and believe that it can do no wrong. That's naive. Even the best-run companies are constantly being tugged in many directions. When the accounting practices of such household-name companies as Cisco and IBM are being questioned, there's no substitute for hard-nosed realism.

"Top management is always trying to put as good a spin on things as possible," says Paul McEntire, a periodic short seller and manager of the Marketocracy Technology Plus mutual fund. "I still believe that the vast majority of executives will be straightforward if you just ask them the right questions. But a case like Enron is going to make people skeptical for a long time to come."

George Anders (ganders@fastcompany.com) runs *Fast Company*'s West Coast bureau from San Francisco.

Five Habits of Highly Reliable Organizations

THE WORST THING ABOUT RECENT BUSINESS SCANDALS IS THEIR LINGERING AFTEREFFECT: HOW CAN YOU MOVE FORWARD WHEN YOU DON'T KNOW WHO YOU CAN DEPEND ON? KARL E. WEICK SAYS THE ANSWER IS INSIDE HIGHLY RELIABLE ORGANIZATIONS. FOR THEM, UNCERTAINTY IS THE "GOOD STUFF."

It is a world after Enron. After the Global Crossing and K-Mart bankruptcies. After accusations of improprieties on Wall Street and irregularities at some of the nation's most storied professional-services firms.

It is a time when businesspeople ask, "Who can we rely on?"—and they are asking with good cause.

The answer comes from an unexpected source: Karl E. Weick, the smartest business thinker you've never heard of. A private, academic noncelebrity who labors at the University of Michigan at Ann Arbor, Weick is revered by such public celebrities as Jim Collins and Tom Peters. And his work—notably, the opaque but groundbreaking 1969 book, The Social Psychology of Organizing—is among the most cited in the sphere of organizational theory.

As an organizational psychologist, Weick has studied the inner workings of everything from firefighting crews to jazz combos. In *Managing the Unexpected: Assuring High Performance in an Age of Complexity* (Jossey-Bass, 2001), Weick and coauthor Kathleen Sutcliffe (also from the University of Michigan) assess what's called "high-reliability organizations"—operations such as aircraft-carrier and nuclear-power-plant crews. High-reliability organizations, or HROs, share two essential characteristics: They constantly confront the unexpected and operate with remarkable consistency and effectiveness.

In the wake of today's business turbulence and, more recently, just plain bad business, Weick's analysis of HROs offers important lessons. His message: The best way for any company—and its people—to respond to unpredictable challenges is by building an effective organization that expertly spots the unexpected when it crops up and then quickly adapts to meet the changed environment. In a series of interviews, Weick revealed the five habits of highly reliable organizations.

1. *Don't be tricked by your success.* HROs don't gloat over their successes. In fact, it's just the opposite: They are preoccupied with their failures. They are incredibly sensitive to their own lapses and errors, which serve as windows into their system's vulnerability. They pick up on small

deviations. And they react early and quickly to anything that doesn't fit with their expectations.

Navy aviators often talk about "leemers," a gut feeling that something isn't right. A pilot feels puzzled, agitated, or anxious. Even though he doesn't know exactly what's wrong, he knows that he needs to abort the mission. Typically, those leemers turn out to be good intuitions: Something, in fact, is wrong.

HROs create climates where people feel safe trusting their leemers. They question assumptions and report problems. They quickly review unexpected events, no matter how inconsequential. They encourage members to be wary of success, suspicious of quiet periods, and concerned about stability and lack of variety, both of which can lead to carelessness and errors.

2. *Defer to your experts on the front line.* There are so many deviations out there, so much dissonance. How do we know what's really worth paying attention to? The answer: Listen to your experts—the people on the front line.

People at the top may think that they have the big picture. More accurately, they have a picture, certainly not the picture, and certainly not bigger in the sense that it includes more data.

The picture that frontline workers see is different. It is drawn from their firsthand knowledge of the company's operations, strengths, and weaknesses. What is important about the frontline workers' view is that these people capture a fuller picture of what the organization faces and what it can actually do. In most cases, they see more chances for bold action than the executives at the top. So it's better for HROs to allow decisions to migrate to frontline expertise rather than to the top of preestablished hierarchies, where positions are often filled for reasons other than experience.

3. *Let the unexpected circumstances provide your solution.* I've written about the Mann Gulch fire that killed 13 smoke jumpers in 1949. In all, it was a tragic organizational failure. But what was amazing was the reaction of the foreman, Wagner Dodge, when the fire was nearly on top of his men. On the spot, he invented the escape fire—a small fire that would consume all of the brush around him and his team, leaving an area where the larger fire couldn't burn.

He acted in a way that was contrary to all of the things that firefighters have habitually done. That's part of being resilient. Put simply, it's about having a steady head.

When something out of the ordinary happens, your stress level rises. The safest prediction for what will happen next is that your perception will narrow—you will get tunnel vision—and you will miss a lot of stuff. You have to be able to resist that dramatic narrowing of cues—because within everything that is happening unexpectedly, you will find what you need for a remedy.

4. *Embrace complexity.* Business is complex, in large part because it is unknowable and unpredictable. In the face of all of this complexity, HROs are reluctant to accept simplification. They understand that it takes complexity to sense complexity.

   We all instinctively try to simplify the data that we receive, but there are better and worse simplifications. Better simplifications arise from a deeper knowledge of the environment along with a deeper understanding of the organization and its capabilities. That knowledge and understanding develops when people attend to more things, entertain a greater variety of interpretations, differentiate their ideas, argue, listen to one another, work to reconcile differences, and commit to revisiting and updating whatever profound simplicities they settle on as guidelines for action.

   A complex organization is made up of diverse people with diverse experience. Its complexity fosters adaptability.

5. *Anticipate—but also anticipate your limits.* We try to anticipate as much as we possibly can. But we can't anticipate everything. There's such a premium on planning, on budgeting, on making the numbers. In the face of all that, the notion of resilience has an affirming quality: You don't have to get it all right in advance.

   Good strategy does not rely on anticipation alone. It's built on a smaller scale, updated more frequently, and driven by actions. You don't present it to your board of directors that way, but it's more useful guidance than the kind you can get from a grander notion of strategy. It's not, Think, then act. Instead, it's, Think by acting. By actually doing things, you'll find out what works and what doesn't.

   That doesn't mean you should stop anticipating. But you should add in two subtleties. First, focus your attention on key mistakes that you do not want to make. Second, trust your anticipations, but be wary of their accuracy. You can't see the whole context that is developing. Your anticipation is probably a reasonable first approximation of what might be happening, but no matter how shrewd you are, it won't cover some key features.

Most important, you should build a capacity for resilience. Life events are indeterminate. We can't fix or know everything. The beauty and the frightening quality of hubris is that people believe they're in the know completely.

I hope that emergency-room doctors, nuclear-power-plant operators, and firefighters know what the hell they're doing. But I don't believe it for a second. How they struggle with that—and how you and I struggle with that—is, for me, the good stuff. That's the human condition.

Keith H. Hammonds (khammonds@fastcompany.com) is a *Fast Company* senior editor. Contact Karl E. Weick by email (karlw@umich.edu).

HOW MINDFUL IS YOUR COMPANY?

In *Managing the Unexpected,* Karl E. Weick and Kathleen Sutcliffe argue that high reliability organizations exhibit "mindfulness." Basically, mindfulness indicates a combination of high alertness, flexibility, and adaptability. Take this quiz to rate your company's mindfulness. Give yourself the following number of points for each of the corresponding statements: 1 point for "Not at all," 2 points for "To some extent," and 3 points for "A great deal."

1. There is an organization wide sense of susceptibility to the unexpected.
2. Everyone feels accountable for reliability.
3. Leaders pay as much attention to managing unexpected events as they do to achieving formal organizational goals.
4. People at all levels of our organization value quality.
5. We have spent time identifying how our activities could potentially harm our organization, employees, customers, other interested parties, and the environment at large.
6. We pay attention to when and why our employees, customers, or other interested parties might feel peeved at or disenfranchised by the organization.
7. There is widespread agreement among the firm's members on what shouldn't go wrong.
8. There is widespread agreement among the firm's members on what could go wrong.

A total score higher than 16 indicates an exemplarily mindful infrastructure in your firm. A score lower than 10 suggests a need for immediate improvement.

DISCUSSION QUESTIONS FOR SECTION 2

1. What is your reaction to the former employees of Enron and their view of the company? Do you think you would have worked for the firm if given the opportunity?

2. What role did Wall Street analysts play in the demise of Enron?

3. Which of the six lessons discussed in the third article do you think is the most important one? Why?

4. How would a company put in place the recommendations proposed in the fourth article?

SOCIAL RESPONSIBILITY

This section examines the responsibility of corporations and not-for-profit (NFP) organizations to society in general. The articles cover a relatively large U.S.–based corporation (Interface), a South African company (Freeplay Group), and a U.S. NFP (Pioneer Human Services).

Much discussion in recent years has focused on corporate social responsibility (CSR). Furthermore, the notion of sustainability, which indicates that companies should focus both on long-term sustainability as well as short-term economic gains, has gained momentum in recent years. These approaches have been institutionalized in a procedure called the "triple bottom line" that reports on the economic, social, and environmental aspects of a company's business. The leading proponents of the "triple bottom line" are bp, Shell, Nestlé, and Six Continents (an international— UK–based—hotel chain that owns Holiday Inn). This notion seems to have best taken hold in Europe thus far.

The first selection in this section discusses Interface and its CEO, Ray Anderson, and his long-standing commitment to environmental stewardship and sustainability. This carpet manufacturer with a number of plants throughout the country has pioneered a better and more environmentally friendly way to make carpets. The other individuals and their stories recounted in this article are a testament to the effectiveness of Ray Anderson's leadership.

The Freeplay Group, which is based in Cape Town, South Africa, has an ambitious agenda. The company wants to both capture the buyer's imagination and change the world. They hope to revolutionize the way a mundane product, radios, are manufactured and sold. Their objective is to create and promote jobs for the disabled in South Africa. With the help of some well-known investors, the company is aiming to make high profits. However, its mission and values are the primary drivers of the organization. Their agenda is to combine innovation with a strong commitment to social justice. With the steadfastness it has demonstrated already, the Freeplay Group is likely to accomplish this ambitious goal. Read "Freeplay Principles" for more details.

The third selection builds on a similar theme as the second article. Pioneer Human Services of Seattle, Washington, is a not-for-profit organization that is involved with some of the largest companies in that area, including Boeing and Starbucks. The Pioneer workforce is made up of former criminal offenders and drug addicts. However, this organization is known for its professionalism and business acumen. Pioneer fosters a "tough love" environment to help these individuals get back on the straight and narrow path. In most cases their efforts are successful, but the end of the article points out that success is not universal. This not-for-profit's (NFP) mission demonstrates that social responsibility can work equally well in an NFP business as in a profit-making one. In conclusion, "The Social Justice Agenda" lays out several key points for a successful agenda emphasizing people as well as performance.

Although numerous examples of CSR (probably a number in your community) exist, these three organizations illustrate that the larger role for organizations in society has taken root around the world. With the many challenges of the 21st century, it is encouraging to see a commitment to societal issues is now receiving increasing attention by both large and small firms, as well as those in the not-for-profit sector domestically and internationally.

BY CHARLES FISHMAN   FROM *FAST COMPANY* ISSUE 14, PAGE 136

Sustainable Growth— Interface, Inc.

RAY ANDERSON OF INTERFACE INC. POINTS THE WAY TO HIGH PROFITABILITY AND ZERO WASTE—A FUTURE THAT MERGES ECONOMIC GROWTH WITH SOCIAL RESPONSIBILITY.

Ray Anderson has spent most of his life as an environmental vandal. He has devoted his career—the better part of four decades—to mastering the black magic of the 20th century: He takes huge lakes of petroleum and spins them into elegant brocades.

The petroleum, which took millions of years to make, is irreplaceable. The brocades—beautiful woven fabrics that carpet offices and corridors from the U.S. Capitol to MTV headquarters—will last forever. After just 10 years, most of that fabric will end up in the dump.

Indeed, Anderson's success has been marked by a kind of galloping envirogluttony. He is the 63-year-old founder and CEO of Interface Inc., an Atlanta-based company with 7,300 employees. Its business: turning petrochemicals into textiles. In 26 factories on four continents, Anderson's looms produce a million pounds of synthetic carpet and fabric every day—along with more than seven tons of air pollutants every year.

Ray Anderson is a certified captain of industrial capitalism. He is also becoming one of the nation's leading environmentalists, a radical who makes the folks from Greenpeace look timid.

Four years ago, Anderson made a decision that changed the course of his carpet company, and that could transform the nation's economy. He decided that Interface would become, as he put it, "the first fully sustainable industrial enterprise, anywhere." Anderson decided that his petrochemical conglomerate would become 100% environmentally benign.

His vision for the 21st century: Interface would no longer use virgin nylon yarn to stitch its fabrics. Interface's factories and offices would use power from renewable sources only. Interface would produce zero waste; indeed, it would reclaim its own products and use them as raw material for new textiles. And Interface would pull its suppliers and customers into its sustainability orbit, insisting that the products it bought be recyclable and nontoxic, pushing clients to think differently about carpeting—and about their own businesses. "I want to pioneer the company of the next industrial revolution," says Ray Anderson.

Anderson wants to turn the entire U.S. economy inside out. He wants to harness the awesome, triumphant engine of democratic capitalism to the task of fixing

47

the environment—before that engine suffocates on its own waste. The concept is simple: For its first century, industrial capitalism has been obliviously, relentlessly linear: raw materials, energy, product, packaging, marketing, waste. In the century to come, Anderson wants business to evolve to the next level: cyclic capitalism. Companies would consume their own waste. Landfills, after all, are best seen as a yardstick of the failure of human ingenuity. In nature, there is no garbage; everyone's waste becomes someone else's food.

Anderson's thinking is so advanced, and the efforts at Interface are so far along, that Interface ranks as the most highly evolved big company in the country today. In terms of combining social responsibility and economic growth, no one comes close. At Interface, social responsibility and growth has become the same thing.

From 1995 to 1996, sales at the publicly traded company grew from $800 million to $1 billion. During that same period, the amount of raw materials used by the company dropped almost 20% per dollar of sales. Which means, says Anderson, "The world just saw the first $200 million of sustainable business."

Interface's performance shatters the idea that environmental stewardship is just another cost. During the first three years of the company's drive toward sustainability, from 1994 to 1997, its net income totaled about $84 million. During that time, the company saved $50 million—in reduced materials costs, reduced energy costs, and reduced waste. That money went to the bottom line, not to the dump.

Of course, you can't reinvent the modern industrial enterprise in just a year or two; it's not that easy to disconnect a giant company from a century's worth of supply arrangements and infrastructural habits. Interface still consumes 10,000 pounds of virgin nylon per hour, still trucks almost 30 tons of garbage to landfills per day, still sends 2.3 million pounds of CO_2 into the air per week.

But a dramatic change has taken hold at the company. From the factory floor to the R&D lab, sustainability has become as important a consideration in every business decision as profitability. Interface, for instance, has developed a new idea about carpeting and customers: It wants to lease carpet instead of selling it. The company would make, install, and maintain the carpet, take it back from customers, and then turn the old carpet into new carpet.

Says John Picard, a corporate environmental consultant who helped Interface develop the leasing idea: "Ray Anderson is going to be one of those people you look back on and say, 'He changed the world.' Interface is the corporation of the 21st century."

NYLON IS FOREVER

The nylon molecule from which interface spins its carpet has two amazing properties: It is completely recyclable, and it is stable for eternity—which is why discarding it by the ton hardly makes sense. Still, there is a small flaw in Ray Anderson's plan to recycle carpet by leasing it and taking it back: Right now, it's neither feasible nor economical to turn carpet back into carpet.

Don Ellison, 50, a preacher-turned-factory manager, is explaining the problem at Interface's plant in West Point, Georgia. "Look at this beam of yarn," he says, pointing to a stainless-steel spool of yarn the size of a truck axle. The shining spool is meticulously wound with half a ton of yarn. "That beam has 205 'ends' of thread," says Ellison. "Five colors form a color pattern of 18 threads, repeated over and over." The 205 ends will be threaded into a large stitching machine and "tufted" into a lovely piece of tan carpeting flecked with turquoise and maroon. "Once you weave all this into carpet, stitched through and backed with latex, you can see the problem," says Ellison. "It's no easy task to take it apart, separate it, and use all those parts again."

True. But if recycling is hard, consider what it takes to make carpet. Helicopter out to the middle of the Gulf of Mexico. Straight down, beneath 750 feet of water and 11,000 feet of bedrock, is an enormous lake of crude oil. Suck up some of that crude, wind it onto Ellison's stainless-steel bobbin, and weave carpet out of it. That's no easy task either. Indeed, seen from that vantage point, making carpet the modern way—using oil rigs, tankers, petroleum-cracking plants, pipelines, and nylon-spinning factories—seems improbable.

That's the shift in perspective that Anderson wants to cultivate. At Interface, the change is happening in two ways. First, across the company, employees are wringing out as much waste as possible. At its plant in LaGrange, Georgia, Interface used to send six tons of carpet trimmings to the landfill every day: ribbons of brand new carpet, made and discarded within hours. By reducing the unnecessarily generous comfort margins built into its production system, the factory has dramatically reduced its scrap. Since June of last year, the plant has sent no trimmings to the landfill. What scrap remains is recycled—much of it back into carpet. Net savings: 3 million pounds a year of indestructible carpet that is not sent to the dump.

At Guilford of Maine, a division of Interface, new computer controls on the boilers in a fabric factory reduced carbon monoxide emissions by 99.7%, from two tons a week to a couple of hundred pounds a year. The computer controls also improved the efficiency of the boilers by 23%, by minimizing human error and by monitoring temperatures more precisely.

Every Interface factory has similar stories. At Bentley Mills—a division in Los Angeles that makes luxurious, high-end carpet—the amount of scrap carpet wasn't even tracked until June 1996. When employees first measured the scrap, they discovered they were throwing away 2 running yards of carpet for every 100 yards they stitched. That's the equivalent of operating the factory two days a year, three shifts a day, and throwing all that carpet away. By the end of 1997, the scrap carpet had been cut by 30%.

The second change sweeping Interface is the company's determination to transform the way carpet is made and sold in the 21st century. At the moment, the Bentley Mills dye house, where carpet yarn gets its vivid colors, is still the kind of factory that Charles Dickens would recognize: cavernous, smelling of ammonia, with cauldrons radiating clouds of steam. Huge carts, stacked with carefully skeined yarn, are lined up everywhere. Some yarn is the whitish gray of raw thread; the rest presents a riot of color—mauve, aqua, tan, blue. The process of giving thread its color hasn't changed in 5,000 years. Put the thread in a pot that contains water and a dyeing agent. Boil it. Dry it.

At the Bentley Mills dye house, the cauldrons can handle 5,000 pounds of yarn at once; 10,000 gallons of water and dye are brought to a boil in a vat big enough to submerge a compact car. The yarn is dried in an oven the size of a small trailer house. It's a system that consumes an enormous amount of energy—and that could never be run on solar panels.

Around the corner in the dye house, workers are using a different method to color yarn. The raw yarn unspools through a couple of glass-enclosed boxes, through a small steam box, and then into a series of drying chambers. Then, fully colored, it spools back onto a cone at the end of the line. In that first set of boxes, dye is sprayed onto the moving strand of yarn. Excess dye is captured and constantly recycled. The steam chamber fixes the dye.

Each drying box is not much larger than a microwave oven. A strand of yarn speeds through it at 1,200 feet per minute.

"This is the first machine of its kind anywhere in the world," says Jim Harley, 39, the vice president of manufacturing at Bentley Mills. Compared with the boil-and-bake method—which, for the time being, Bentley Mills will continue to use at least partially—"this system uses 10% of the energy," says Harley. "Or less. At half the cost. And with this system, there is no wastewater or dye going into the sewer." And this system could run on solar panels.

The most visible step toward the kind of cyclic, sustainable company that Anderson envisions was taken at Interface's Guilford of Maine division. Guilford specializes in making the fabric that upholsters cubicles. Using fabric made from polyester fiber, which is delivered in 600-pound bales from a supplier, Interface upholsters half the office cubicles in the country.

"We've always used virgin polyester fiber," says Paul Paydos, 46, Guilford's vice president of technical services. But Guilford decided to produce cubicle fabric from recycled polyester—which had to be indistinguishable from the virgin polyester fabric in quality and price. It took about a year to make the change.

With the bargaining muscle that comes with making 15 million running yards of fabric a year, Guilford partnered with a South Carolina soda-bottle-recycling outfit to supply the plant with recycled polyester fiber that is chemically identical to the virgin product. Last June, Guilford looms started using the recycled polyester; by the end of the year, all the cubicle fabric was woven from old soda bottles.

Now Guilford is working with suppliers on an even more advanced step. "Our goal is to throw discarded cubicle fabric back in the smoking cauldron," Paydos says, "and have new polyester raw material come out."

PLANTING THE NEW ECONOMY

Ray Berard is a senior vice president in Interface's R&D division, overseeing a dozen efforts to design carpet and fabric that can be pulled apart and turned into carpet again. But for Berard, a 60-year-old with a PhD in physical chemistry, who has worked at Celanese Corp. and Titleist & FootJoy Worldwide, one the most exciting projects involves all-natural commercial carpet.

"It's made of hemp," Berard says, "backed with natural fiber, using natural dyes. It looks good, and it feels good." To make the point, he displays a square sample located behind his desk. "And it has wicked strength," he says. Hemp "grows so fast, it keeps the weeds out. You don't need pesticides or herbicides. And when you're done with the carpet, you can take it, compost it completely, and use it to fertilize the next crop of hemp."

The only problem: Growing industrial hemp in the United States is illegal, because of its genetic relation to marijuana. For now, Berard is looking to Canada and Asia for supplies of hemp—he's already bought the harvest from 150 acres—and he hopes to start offering commercial hemp carpet later this year.

Berard's projects are part of the new world that Anderson envisions. They represent a radical leap from the way business is done now—involving different relationships and different ways of thinking about suppliers, customers, products, garbage, and raw material. But as Interface is proving every day, that world is very much within reach: Lease carpet instead of selling it—progress begins with an idea just that simple.

The human economy doesn't have to be the only one on Earth that generates garbage. Cyclic capitalism—a form of business that refreshes itself and the world around it—would fire the imaginations of those who make the current, more primitive capitalism thrive. And as Anderson says, "It's the right thing to do."

Charles Fishman cnfish@mindspring.com is a *Fast Company* contributing editor. You can visit Interface Inc. on the Web at http://www.ifsia.com

The Agenda—Social Justice

THE FREEPLAY GROUP, BASED IN CAPE TOWN, SOUTH AFRICA, BUILDS PRODUCTS THAT CAPTURE THE IMAGINATION OF THE WORLD—AND THAT CHANGE THE WORLD.

The Freeplay Group, a young, fast-growing company based in Cape Town, South Africa, wants to build products that capture the imagination of the world. It also wants to change the world—which means it has to operate in many different worlds. January in Las Vegas: Hundreds of thousands of businesspeople and technology geeks have gathered for the annual International Consumer Electronics Show. Even by Las Vegas standards, the show is a spectacle. A maze of booths sprawls across more than 1 million square feet of convention space. Some 1,800 companies are competing for the attention of the attendees. There is glitz—and schlock—galore: Three people in six-foot-tall, rhinestone-bedecked parrot suits dance to a company jingle; a bright-red sports car provides a place to demo new speakers. The whole scene is set to a bone-shaking hip-hop beat—the music of choice to showcase new audio technology.

Freeplay doesn't have to shout for attention. The company's booth is lined with a collection of stylish, transparent radios in eye-pleasing colors: wild cherry, lime, blueberry. They look as if they've been carved from giant Lifesaver candies. Each radio has a handle that, when wound up, generates the power to play the radio. There are no electric cords and no batteries. People can play these "self-powered" devices, which sell for $79.95, for free—hence the name.

"What's this?" asks a curious visitor, clad in a black T-shirt and jeans. "An iMac radio?" A Freeplay staffer hands him a device. "Wind it up," she says. The man folds out the handle and turns it for 10 seconds. The chorus from "Zoot Suit Riot," by Cherry Poppin' Daddies, blasts from the speaker. The base of the handle, now retracted snugly against the radio's face, spins slowly backward as the gears—visible from the outside—turn kinetic energy into electricity. "This is incredibly cool," he says. "Where can I buy one?"

Meanwhile, an ocean away, in a tin-shack classroom in the South African province of KwaZulu-Natal, a Freeplay radio is attracting eager attention from a very different audience. A group of kids is crowding around for an English lesson. In this part of KwaZulu-Natal, Zulu is the primary language, and electricity is a luxury, not a utility. Few residents can afford to buy batteries. And few teachers are fluent in English. Enter the Freeplay radio, donated by War Child, an aid organization based in London. War Child has purchased enough self-powered radios to help 150,000 South African children to learn English. Every morning, the kids listen to a 30-minute lesson that's broadcast over the radio. Each lesson begins with music and dancing and then moves on to storytelling. The students—ages five through seven—follow along in bright-colored workbooks. "In the rural communities we serve, when the batteries die, the learning stops," says Gordon Naidoo, who coordinates the program. "When we implement the program with these radios, it is instantly sustainable."

Plenty of companies aspire to make money and also to make a difference. Freeplay has delivered on both of those aspirations in dramatic fashion. The company was formed in 1995, shipped its first product in 1996, has generated revenues of $20 million as of March 1999—and expects to reach $35 million by 2000. Freeplay's investors include General Electric Pension Trust; WorldSpace, a satellite-broadcasting company in Washington, DC; and Liberty Life, a top South African insurance company. The company's famous advocates include Nelson Mandela (who made an appearance at a Freeplay factory opening) and Jimmy Carter. Gordon Roddick, chairman of the Body Shop, serves on the board of the Freeplay Foundation. And Terry Waite, the former envoy of the Archbishop of Canterbury, who was held hostage in Beirut, is a trustee of the Freeplay Foundation.

Waite has a decidedly personal connection to Freeplay's flagship product: "I know what being cut off from communication is like. I spent five years in captivity, four of them in solitary confinement, during which time I got no news from the outside world. But near the end of my imprisonment, I did get a small, battery-operated radio. I was terrified that when the batteries died, the guards would not replace them, and I'd be back in total isolation. There are millions of people in this world who are in similar situations—cut off from the flow of information."

So although Freeplay's products have made a big splash in the rich countries—its radios (along with the Freeplay Lantern, a self-powered flashlight that retails for $69.95) are available at RadioShack, the Sports Authority, REI, the Sharper Image, and Harrods, the London retailer—the radios are actually making a difference in the poorest countries. The United Nations Development Program used them to broadcast election results to the people of Liberia; the government of Ghana purchased 30,000 radios so that villagers there could also listen to the elections. War Child may distribute radios to refugees in Zaire, to warn them about land mines in that strife-torn country. And Rotary International plans to use the radios to broadcast information about a child-immunization project in India.

In short, Freeplay is setting the agenda for how to combine the quest for innovation with a commitment to social justice. And its corporate agenda keeps expanding. "We're not just in the radio business," insists Rory Stear, 40, the company's cochairman and co-CEO. "We are in the energy business." Stear, who stands 6'7", has the appeal of an evening news anchor—wavy brown hair, light-blue eyes, a 10,000-watt smile. "We always ask ourselves, What else can we do with this technology? Countries like India have daily power outages. Even if you're a billionaire, you'll need some kind of self-powered device when the lights go out. We're creating a whole new industry that can improve people's lives, whether they're in Los Angeles or Lagos."

"We want to see self-powered products in every village and every city in the world," adds Christopher Staines, 38, Stear's cochair and co-CEO at Freeplay. "This self-powered technology is relevant, whether you're listening to a radio in Botswana, using a laptop computer in New Jersey, or hiking the mountains of Peru with a global-positioning system. That's our goal."

COMMITMENT TO INNOVATION

The workroom on the second floor of Freeplay's engineering division in Cape Town looks like it's been ransacked: Boxes of parts are strewn about, opened or toppled over. Gears, circuit boards, and springs are piled on room-long counters and on the island workspace. The chaos reflects the crushing deadlines that the six-person team had to meet for Freeplay to make a splash at the International Consumer Electronics Show. Several of the engineers worked well past midnight on Christmas Eve, building the prototypes of the FPR3 that Freeplay displayed in Vegas. The team now has just three weeks to debug the prototypes and prepare the specs for the factory.

Inside each radio lies the heart of Freeplay's proprietary technology—a spring made of a two-inch-wide, 20-foot-long ribbon of carbonized steel. The spring is positioned so that turning the handle forces it to wind backward onto a bobbin. The force of the spring rewinding itself drives a set of gears, which in turn feed into an electric generator—a DC (direct current) motor powered in reverse. The electricity feeds from the generator into a circuit board, which regulates the rate of unwinding. Winding for 30 seconds produces up to an hour of playing time on the radio and generates about 3 minutes of light from the flashlight.

Chris Rhomberg, the team's lone electrical engineer, has been hunched over the FPR3's circuit board for two days. The sales team in Las Vegas noticed that at higher volumes, the sound from the radio was distorted. Rhomberg, 30, is working on the problem. Meanwhile, Gavin de Bres, 30, and James Ramsey, who at 36 is the oldest team member, are building rough prototypes for a new project: One of the world's biggest toy companies has asked Freeplay to submit a proposal for a self-powered mechanism for a miniature monster truck that, when finished, will be a brilliantly simple device, powered by a spring that is wound up by pushing the truck backward. Three revs and it will roar off, no batteries required. For the moment, though, the truck is only a klunky, open aluminum box with the spring and gears bolted inside.

This workshop-clubhouse has no private offices. The engineers spend their time in perpetual motion, touching base for 30 seconds here, or two minutes there, swapping information, asking a question, and then returning to their piece of the project. Watching the team work is like seeing professional volleyball players in action—everyone touches the ball, and it never hits the floor. It's easy to understand how this group designed and produced the current version of the Freeplay radio in just 14 weeks.

Rhomberg, who's been quietly assembling the case of the radio that he's been debugging, interrupts the group's conversation. "Listen to this," he says. He winds up the radio and cranks up the volume. The music spills out—loud and clear. Everyone knows what that means—the bug is out. Fellow team member Pierre Becker thumps Rhomberg on his back as the rest of the group applauds. "Take that, Sony!" Becker says.

That kind of tenacity is precisely what John Hutchinson, Freeplay's director of engineering, wants to cultivate. Hutchinson, a shaggy-haired 46-year-old, has a laid-back, informal management style. But there are two kinds of people he won't toler-ate—"liars and loners." At some point, every member of his design team has weathered a verbal thrashing from Hutchinson over those issues. Hutchinson com-bines the meticulousness of an engineer with the doggedness of a lawyer, and, in fact, he has degrees in both fields, as well as an MBA. "For us—working with these tight product cycles and inventing new technology as we go—it has to be about team-work," he says. "We can't have one guy work on the design and then hand it to the mechanical guy, who drops it in the lap of the electronics guy. It has to be seamless collaboration from the start. And if you screw something up, by God, you'd better say so. It's okay to make a mistake, but we can fix it a lot faster if you open up the mistake to the group."

In exchange for his demands, Hutchinson offers a huge amount of freedom. The company has box seats at the national rugby games, and Hutchinson rotates tickets among team members. He also takes team members up in his ultralight plane, a pas-sion that he's had since the 1980s, when he built his own makeshift rig from a hang glider and a chain-saw motor. To Hutchinson, flying is the perfect model for the team's working relationship. "Once you're in the air, it doesn't matter who the hell you are or what your title is. You're totally exposed. You have to trust each other."

Not only do Freeplay engineers have to trust each other, they also have to trust in the technology's potential. This small, resource-strapped company has taken on some big-time risks. The company is feverishly developing self-powered prod-ucts—a global-positioning system, a land-mine detector, a water purifier—for which there is no proven market. The purifier is particularly ingenious: When water and salt are combined in the prototype's metal cup, the machine produces enough hypochlorite to sanitize 10 liters of water. Its potential is vast: It could purify water supplies in disaster areas; it might even prevent the spread of AIDS by generating clean water to mix with powdered infant formula. (One source of infection is communal breast-feeding.)

"We have a real sense of commitment," says Hutchinson. "It comes from doing honest work, for an honest wage, to make a product that's meaningful. The Red Cross, for instance, gave radios to a village in Afghanistan. One little boy had the job of winding the radio. The whole village would gather to listen to the radio; it was an incredibly important part of their community. One day, the boy accidentally broke the handle. He was so distraught that he ran away from home! If that story doesn't teach us the importance of quality, nothing will."

Chris Rhomberg sums up the sentiment this way: "We're like a family that works together." That philosophy is reinforced by the Afrikaans phrase that the engi-neers use when answering their cell phones: Ja, boet. Hello, brother.

MONEY AND MISSION

Breakthrough innovations—from the Apple Mac to the PalmPilot—usually begin with a simple idea that redefines people's expectations about what a product can do.

But even the most brilliant idea requires staying power—the wherewithal to handle the kinds of setbacks and slowdowns that are part of the entrepreneurial process. Stear and Staines have had a lot to do with Freeplay's stamina. The two of them figured out early on how to marry a powerful idea to deep pockets—and still maintain the company's original vision.

Chris Staines remembers precisely when he first encountered the idea that led to that vision. It was April 15, 1994. Staines, who lived in London at the time, was flipping through TV channels while waiting for his wife, Emma, to get ready for an evening out. He stumbled across a BBC show, called "Tomorrow's World," that profiled Trevor Bayliss, the inventor of a wind-up radio. Bayliss built the rig after learning that one of the biggest hurdles in slowing the spread of AIDS in Africa was the inability to inform people in remote regions about safe sex. Bayliss, a blustery, optimistic sort, figured his contraption could do the job—if he could find a partner to build it.

Staines wanted to be that partner. The British native was a finance whiz who'd honed his skills while working in Australia and Britain for the accounting firm known then as Deloitte, Haskins & Sells, and as head of mergers and acquisitions for Seff Corporate Finance in Cape Town. "It was just a brilliant idea," says Staines. "Anyone who couldn't see that was foolish. I had the contacts in South Africa and in the U.K. I knew how to raise money, and I lived less than 100 miles from Bayliss. I couldn't think of one reason why I wasn't the best person to help."

Apologizing to his wife, who was by now ready to go, Staines called Rory Stear in Johannesburg. Staines had worked for Stear for three months at Seff. The two made a great team: Staines, an accountant by training, is as reserved as Stear is gregarious. Stear, a serial entrepreneur, started his first business as a disc jockey at age 18. Staines is more the passionate tactician. "I'm no great humanitarian," he quips. "I suppose I'm an accountant with a vision."

Stear shared Staines's enthusiasm for the radio, so Staines called the BBC and got Bayliss's fax number. That night, Staines stayed awake writing a business plan, which he faxed to Bayliss the next morning. Bayliss agreed to meet for brunch, and a few days later, the three had an agreement. Although Staines and Stear intended to raise money to launch the product, they didn't expect to be doing business with some of the biggest companies in their country and the world. Nor did they intend to run a multimillion-dollar operation with two factories and 270 employees. "We're like the dog that catches the bus," jokes Stear. "What do we do with it now?"

What they did was to build a company. On the wall of the conference room in Freeplay's Cape Town headquarters are copies of cartoons that Stear and Staines commissioned as gifts for their major investors. In each illustration, there is a caricature of Stear on his knees pleading and one of Staines brandishing the Freeplay radio. Also in each cartoon is the investor, appearing either pleased or panicked (depending on how you read the expression) but nevertheless signing a check or showering the founders with cash.

Freeplay's first big check wasn't an investment per se—it was a donation. Stear and Staines were called to a meeting with Andy Bearpark, a former aide to

Margaret Thatcher and the head of humanitarian affairs at the Overseas Development Administration (ODA) in London. ODA gave the partners Pounds150,000 (the equivalent of $235,000 at the time of the transaction, in 1995) to make a commercially viable model of Bayliss's original prototype (which took two minutes to wind and played for only eight minutes) that would be used by aid groups. "It was unbelievably easy to raise funds at first," Stear says. "We did not even have a product yet, but the idea was so compelling that groups like ODA were willing to finance it. The BBC even shot a documentary about us—before we had a factory. It was all very heady and exciting."

One of the people who heard the buzz about the company, which was then called BayGen (as in Bayliss Generator), was Hylton Appelbaum, head of philanthropy of Liberty Life, a big South African insurance company. Appelbaum, 45, was intrigued by the radio's potential in Africa, a place filled with people who had no access to electricity. The Liberty Life Foundation offered the company Pounds1 million (about $238,000 in 1995) to build its marketing operation.

But the money didn't last long. Realizing that Freeplay could not outsource its manufacturing (its production runs were too short), Stear went back to Appelbaum for additional funding for a factory. The Liberty Life Foundation's primary goals were to promote job creation and to assist the disabled. Appelbaum saw a chance to address both goals through Freeplay. He offered another Pounds1.7 million (or $480,000)—not to the company but to a consortium of nonprofit organizations for the disabled. This consortium then gave the money to Freeplay to open a factory. The consortium took a 50% interest in the factory, Liberty Life Foundation got a 25% stake, and the workers got 25%. Freeplay got board control and full management responsibility. A year later, Freeplay used the same financial structure to open a factory to manufacture flashlights. This time the key stakeholder was NICRO (National Institute for Crime Prevention and the Reintegration of Offenders), an organization that helps ex-convicts and abused women.

"It was a perfect investment," Appelbaum says. "We were able to create jobs for people who had the least chance of getting them, while helping to decrease crime. And we did it in a sustainable way."

The next crucial investor was Gordon Roddick, who visited Freeplay's factory and was impressed: "Thousands of good ideas die because the right people are not there to carry them out," says Roddick. "Rory and Chris were entrepreneurial—hungry. They were also taken with the idea of creating a socially responsible business. My visit coincided with their first big cash shortage, so I became an investor."

Over the next two years, Roddick invested more than $2 million. He also provided a virtual blank check as overdraft security on Freeplay's production. (Which is why Roddick's cartoon depicts him galloping in on a white horse.) "At one time, Gordon owned 42,000 radios," Stear marvels. "He'd buy them at cost, we'd stockpile them and sell them when we could. For a while, Gordon was the world's largest collector of wind-up radios."

But Freeplay's vision was too expansive to be financed by a single investor. So in 1997, it wooed its first big-time corporate investor, the General Electric Pension

Trust. In return for a one-third stake, GE provided $11 million. The deal also included a research partnership with GE, whose labs in Schenectady, New York had been working on self-powered technology. The cartoon marking this investment shows Leonard Fassler, head of GE Pension Trust, suspended midshot over a basketball hoop—Michael Jordan-style—tossing an armful of cash through the hoop into Stear's arms.

"Ultimately," says Stear, "we all want to make startlingly good profits. GE didn't invest because it wanted to feel good. It invested because it was getting in on a major industry, and it expects to realize extraordinary returns on the investment. We're not asking for charity. This is a commercial venture. But if you can make a huge profit and make a difference, that's nice."

MANUFACTURING VALUES

Freeplay's manufacturing facilities are a 20-minute drive north of headquarters. The verdant route, lined with South African pines, winds past the University of Cape Town and the Groote Schuur Hospital, where Dr. Christiaan Barnard performed the world's first heart transplant. The ride offers a scenic view of Table Mountain and lush hills covered in soft green bush that the Afrikaners call fynbros. It is an unusual plant—as are the plants in which Freeplay builds its radios and flashlights. In one, a third of the 125 workers are blind, deaf, paraplegic, or otherwise handicapped. In the other, half of the 125 workers are ex-convicts or battered women. With the exception of the occasional wheelchair, it's impossible to tell the disabled from the able-bodied, the criminals from the victims.

Freeplay executives shrug at the idea that they are conducting a bold social experiment inside their factories. When the assembly lines opened two years ago, 125 people produced 500 radios per day. Today the same number of people make 2,000 radios per day. The output per person is the same in the factory with handicapped workers as it is in the factory without them. Both factories have defect rates of less than 1%.

Given the specialized, labor-intensive nature of its assembly process, it's tough to benchmark Freeplay's productivity against that of other factories with processes that are more automated. But it's easy to gauge the commitment of the workers. "Our factory is across a four-lane highway from the bus stop where many of the workers get off," explains Derek Sturgess, 51, Freeplay's manufacturing director. "A couple of months into our first production run, I got a call from a local traffic cop who told me about two of our blind employees who were stuck without a sighted person to help them cross the road. The bus pulled away, and the two men just took off across the street. A five-car pileup resulted! When I asked the men about the incident, they said they were determined to be on time."

Maxwell Khosana, 28, has been working at Freeplay for seven months, installing motors in the radios. Khosana flunked his high school exams in 1991, and, shortly after that, his mother lost her job. Faced with no job prospects and a younger brother to feed, Khosana was easily recruited by some friends to break into houses. During an attempted robbery, one of Khosana's cohorts assaulted a worker who had been painting the house targeted for the break-in. The worker later died, and Khosana spent five years in prison. Afterward he worked for a short time in a bakery and in a restaurant, both of which eventually went broke. Then he heard about NICRO, which led him to a job at Freeplay.

"When I arrived here, I was shocked," Khosana says. "In my previous jobs, you had to call the boss 'mister' or 'sir.' Here, I am told there is no boss, that I am in charge of me. I stopped feeling like I was going to die. This job gave me back my dignity. Even people in my community—they look at me now, and they respect me. They don't see a criminal. They see someone who made a mistake. Freeplay made me feel like a person when I felt less than that."

Hylton Applebaum, the person who envisioned the factories as they are today, couldn't be more satisfied with the results. "I get goose bumps," he says. "I took a friend of mine who is disabled to see the plant. His first thought was, 'It's a sheltered environment where people are patronized and given special treatment.' But he saw that it wasn't like that at all. At the end of the day, we were standing outside the factory next to stacks of boxes labeled, 'Made in South Africa.' And his eyes filled with tears. You can't imagine how significant and inspiring the work done in the factory is."

To Staines, the factories are flesh-and-blood examples of the value system that drives his company—but they are merely a part of the social impact that he wants Freeplay to make. "Our larger vision involves how the products are used, not just how they're made," he says. "When we employ several hundred workers in South Africa, we touch some lives. But when we ship 5,000 radios into a community—and then the radios get used to teach about health care, AIDS, agriculture—we are giving thousands of people a chance to better themselves. That's what keeps me going."

Adds Rory Stear: "I don't want to preach to anybody about how to do things. I just do what makes sense for me as a person and for our business. But when I come to the Unites States, I am overwhelmed by its abundance and by how isolated Americans are from the rest of the world. I just don't believe that talented people can pursue wealth in a vacuum. There's no reason why U.S. companies can't be doing things similar to what we're doing—even inside the United States. Sure we want above-average financial returns, but we also want to feel good about what we are doing."

Not all of Freeplay's partners feel as good about the company's social vision as the company's co-CEOs do. Indeed, Stear worries that, to some people, Freeplay's values come off as soft-headed—or worse, as calculated self-promotion. That's why he is now working so hard to get through to Freeplay's distributors and retailers that are in wealthy countries. These are the places that he hopes will not only buy the company's products but also buy into its worldview.

Back in Las Vegas, Stear hosts a dinner during the International Consumer Electronics Show. His guest of honor is one of the company's most important U.S. reps. This rep has owned a distribution network on the West Coast for more than 20 years. He's the guy who put Freeplay in the Sharper Image, and he's one of the people

FREEPLAY PRINCIPLES

The Freeplay Group is setting the agenda for how to combine the quest for innovation with a commitment to social justice. Its cochairmen and co-CEOs, Rory Stear and Christopher Staines, don't apologize for their ambitious business plans and savvy approaches to marketing. Nor will they compromise on their goal to make a difference as well as to make money for their shareholders. Here are some of the principles that are guiding the company's growth.

1. Big problems demand big ambitions.

"We're not just in the radio business," insists Rory Stear. "We are in the energy business." The company's self-powered radios and flashlights are hits, but it keeps searching for new ways to apply its proprietary technology—even when there's no immediate demand for it. Freeplay engineers are experimenting with everything from wind-up laptops to global-positioning systems.

2. Mission matters.

"We're not just a business," says Stear. "We're a business with a soul." It would be easy for Freeplay to leverage its popularity with First World consumers by postponing its plans to distribute radios throughout the Third World. If it did, the company would be more profitable—and even more attractive to investors. But it would lose something valuable as a result—its mission. That's why the young company has already established the Freeplay Foundation, which supplies radios at steep discounts and works with broadcasters to create educational and instructional programming. "We are investing in the future," says Staines. "Not everyone may understand some of the decisions we have made, but those choices will bear fruit in the long term."

(Continued)

who will help the company to expand into sports retailers. He knows his business. But he does not know Freeplay—not really. Looking very much the part of the tough businessman, he lays out Freeplay's challenge as he sees it. "What it comes down to, Rory," he says, gesturing with his bread roll, "is that if you want three feet of shelf space in sporting goods departments, you have to knock someone else out of the way. It's all about killing the competition and ripping their livers out."

One of Stear's young salespeople savors the phrase. "Rip their livers out!" he repeats, "like Hannibal the Cannibal." He waggles his tongue and slurps loudly, mimicking the character from The Silence of the Lambs. The people at the table shriek with laughter. Stear laughs too, but hesitantly. The man is a great partner, but Stear feels that he doesn't "get" what the company is about. "The opportunity to learn from him is immense," Stear confides. "He's got 20 years of experience in retail, and he knows what he's doing. But we won't ever be about profit at all costs. It's hard to get that through to some people."

FREEPLAY PRINCIPLES

3. Small companies need big-name supporters.

With revenues of $20 million as of March 1999, Freeplay is an entrepreneurial success—and still a pip-squeak by most standards. But the company's influence and visibility far exceed its current size. One reason is that it has managed to affiliate itself with big companies, such as General Electric, as well as with big-name humanitarians, such as Terry Waite. "We have gathered the most powerful people we know," says Staines. "It's impossible to measure the value of their contributions."

4. Companies that do good works attract great talent.

"Whether you're running a company with 3 people or 300,000 people," says Stear, "you have to hire the best engineers, the best marketers, the best production workers. The products we make, the programs we have, the mission we espouse make people feel good about working here. Our values become a motivator."

5. Companies can't succeed in countries that fail.

Freeplay has lots of strategic challenges to overcome—raising money, cracking upscale retailers in rich countries, working with aid agencies to distribute radios in poor countries. So why take on the extra challenge of staffing its factories with ex-cons? "Crime is the single-biggest obstacle to the success of a democratic South Africa," says Stear. "Business here can't just pay lip service to stopping crime. And the only way to begin to stop crime is to create jobs. If our company can do that, then so can a whole lot of other companies."

Later that night after the dinner has been eaten, the wine drunk, and the whiskey poured, the rep stands up to say good-bye. He extends his hand to Stear and smiles. "It's been a pleasure," the rep says. "I look forward to furthering your education." Stear shakes his hand. "Thank you," he says graciously. "And I look forward to furthering yours."

Cheryl Dahle (cdahle@fastcompany.com) is a *Fast Company* senior writer. Learn more about Freeplay on the Web (http://www.freeplay.net) or contact Rory Stear (stearbpg@iafrica.com) and Christopher Staines (staines@iafrica.com) by email.

Social Justice— Pioneer Human Services

"WE'VE GOT TWO BOTTOM LINES—THE MONEY AND THE MISSION."

Not many corporate vice presidents can tell the kinds of stories that Marla Gese can.

Gese—a handsome woman with neatly bobbed brown hair, who is wearing a perfectly tailored pantsuit and tasteful diamond earrings—sits sipping coffee in a nondescript beige conference room. As she speaks, it's hard to imagine her living the kind of life that she describes as her past: freebasing enough cocaine to stay awake for 12 days straight, selling a kilo of drugs a day to support her habit, and hiding her stash in the floor of her Datsun. She was arrested five times during an 18-month period and eventually spent 5 years in prison on drug-related charges stemming from a police sting at her house. "It was terrifying," she recalls. "They busted down the doors and came in shouting." She leans across the table and presses two manicured fingernails to the temple of her listener. "Freeze, motherf***er!" she says in a whispered imitation of a cop's command. "That's really true. They really do say that. And you're thinking, 'Jesus, there's a gun pointed to my head!' It's scary stuff."

That's one story from Gese's past. Here's another: Gese, now 40, spent the past six years working her way up from receptionist to vice president of real-estate asset management at Pioneer Human Services, the company that hired her after she got out of jail. As a rent collector and a property manager, she managed to turn around several sites that were losing money in the company's real-estate division and then went on to found Pioneer's construction-services division. What began as a crew of 2 men who worked on 30 Pioneer-owned properties has grown into a team of 45 employees who spend about half of their time bidding for commercial work, such as plumbing and roofing jobs.

"There hasn't been a single challenge that she hasn't been able to meet," says Mike Burns, 57, president and CEO of Pioneer. "She is the perfect example of the amazing things that people can do when they're given a second chance."

Gese's work is also an example of the amazing things that Pioneer has accomplished by giving people like her a second chance. Pioneer is a Seattle-based nonprofit that brings in annual revenues of roughly $52 million. Its mission is to provide employment training, housing, and counseling services to ex-convicts and former drug abusers. Less than 1% of the company's funds come from "charity." The remaining 99% is generated by the 12 divisions that the company runs (among them, sheet-metal factories, catering services, real-estate management, and product-distribution facilities)—the same divisions that provide jobs for ex-offenders and recovering addicts. Each of these individual businesses averages an annual return of 13%, which is reinvested in the company. Pioneer is one of the largest self-sustaining nonprofits in the country. But more mind-boggling than the company's financial success is the paradox that is fueling its growth: Pioneer has succeeded as a business by employing society's most marginalized people, many of whom have been deemed unemployable by other companies.

Pioneer measures its success in two ways. It is not enough to be the primary supplier of cargo liners for Boeing, or to run the swank Mezza Cafe inside the Seattle-based headquarters of Starbucks, or to be the distribution-repackaging center of choice for Hasbro. While serving its corporate customers, Pioneer also serves its internal customers—the more than 6,000 former criminal offenders and drug addicts who receive Pioneer's help each year, in the form of job training, employment, low-income housing, outpatient counseling, and inpatient treatment. "We've got two bottom lines—the money and the mission," Burns says. "We give the people who work here a chance to change their lives."

Before joining Pioneer in March 1999, Burns spent 20 years working as a CEO for such traditional companies as Sea Watch International Inc. and Dutch Boy Paints. His roots are not in social service but in the Marine Corps. (He still wears his shoes polished to a high gloss and his hair parted with military precision.) Given his career background and deceptively reserved demeanor, Burns's passion for his new work might surprise some folks. But perhaps it's his establishment-centered background that makes him appreciate what Pioneer accomplishes every day.

"When I first got a call from a headhunter about Pioneer, I wasn't interested," says Burns. "I thought that it was just a bunch of social workers trying to run a business." The headhunter persisted until Burns finally agreed to fly in and meet the management team. "I toured the facilities, and I was impressed," he says. "This was a real business that was putting out real products, and the management team was as good as any that I'd ever worked with.

"The level of professionalism at Pioneer is equal to—and in some cases, better than—that of the companies I've worked at," Burns continues. "Pioneer has a sincere desire for employees to learn new things. And employees are determined to make the company as good as it can be—in part, because of what the company has done for them."

By embracing its dual goals, Pioneer is creating a new agenda for the way that nonprofits fund their programs. It's a business agenda that eagerly embraces competition and free markets. The company is also forging a new social agenda: Every new account or contract that Pioneer wins gives the company an opportunity to showcase its employees in a new light—not as past offenders but as a productive, and largely untapped, workforce.

TO BUILD THE BUSINESS, BUILD THE PEOPLE

It took Schwanda Taylor about two years to work up the courage to operate the water-jet cutting machine in Pioneer's cargo-liner factory. The machine—a hulking, computerized monster that weighs more than 5 tons—is used for the precision cutting of metals, plastics, and fiberglass. It slices through any material (including six inches of titanium) without leaving any burrs, or rough edges. It works like this: Once a cutting pattern is programmed into the machine, jets of water as narrow as human hairs apply 60,000 pounds of pressure per square inch to cut through whatever substance is being fed into the machine. The device could easily slice off a finger or two in the process.

"At first, I didn't think that I could run the water jet," says Taylor, a soft-spoken woman who, at 34, could pass for a teenager. "But one day, I opened my eyes and thought, 'I've got to stop being scared. I've got to rise above my fears: That's what this place is about.'"

Taylor has conquered many fears since coming to Pioneer. She joined the company through a prerelease program at Washington Corrections Center for Women, at Gig Harbor, where she was serving a five-year sentence on drug-related charges. The pre-release program is one of Pioneer's most successful initiatives. Over a six-year period, it has cut the recidivism rate in half (it's now down to 11% for the women enrolled). And of the 50 women who were released from prison over a two-year period, 100% are still employed. For six months, Taylor took a bus to the factory each morning and returned to the prison each night. Her earnings, after housing payments to the state, were set aside for her in a savings account.

Once released, she decided to continue with Pioneer by taking courses—on company time—that Pioneer offered. She completed the training and participated in one of the quarterly graduation ceremonies that have become legendary at Pioneer. During those events, the company shuts down the factory floor to honor employees' myriad achievements, from the completion of training programs to workplace promotions.

"It was awesome," Taylor says with a wide, genuine smile. "I still get tears in my eyes when I think about that day. I passed every single class on time, and I didn't have to go back and retake a single test. Before every test, I would go into the bathroom and pray. I'd say, 'Lord, you know that I've worked very hard for this. Please let me pass this test.'" Having mastered the water-jet cutter, Taylor now trains other workers on the proper way to use it and other machines as well. The skill has become one more toehold that keeps her from slipping back into her past life.

So that's what Pioneer did for Taylor, but what does a worker like Taylor contribute to Pioneer? For most of last year, she was part of a team that completely restructured Pioneer's cargo-liner factory. The processes, the floor layout, the documentation, the quality inspection—all of those things were reinvented by the workers themselves. "We could not have done it without them," says Dave Meisinger, 48, former vice president for manufacturing operations at Pioneer. A veteran of the electronics-manufacturing industry,

Meisinger has supervised many conversions to team-based production systems, which rely on suggestions from frontline workers to make operations more efficient and to raise output quality. He says that despite some of Pioneer's unique challenges, the company's successful conversion measures up to other efforts that he's supervised in the private sector.

"A lot of people who work here don't have the education or the experience that people at for-profits do," says Meisinger. "But the creativity level here is higher than that of any similar project team that I've worked with. People have come up with solutions to problems that are more advanced than those you might have gotten from for-profit employees. I think that is partly because the employees here truly love having the chance to think freely and to have their input matter. Instead of feeling like a number, they feel like part of a team."

And the results for Pioneer? Cycle time was cut in half. Quality increased by 40%. Even better, the reorganization has freed up space in the warehouse so that Pioneer can manage inventory for its customers. "We can now store finished inventory and spoon-feed it to customers on demand," Meisinger says. "Customers don't have to count inventory, inspect it, or move it around. It's always where they need it, when they need it."

Those improvements would be a great leap for any factory, let alone for a non-profit operation. But historically, the performance level at Pioneer has always been high. The company was the first nonprofit in the country to become ISO-9002 certified, a quality rating that it has maintained since 1996. Such performance is particularly impressive given that the employee turnover rate has been as high as 50%—on purpose. Pioneer shoots for high turnover, because it means that the company is training employees well enough to snare higher-paying jobs in the private sector. Leaving is the pinnacle of recovery for Pioneer's clients, but it is also a thorny challenge for the company. "When someone leaves, you laugh and cry at the same time," Meisinger says. "But it's so rewarding to witness those transformations. You have people with checkered pasts and lots of problems. And then you see this change take place as they work through issues of sobriety and develop work skills. Self-esteem starts to rise, and eventually the employees say, 'I'm ready to try my wings.' Then they fly out of here."

Pioneer copes with its high turnover rate by using a structured and elaborate training system. "We've done a pretty good job of establishing a formal infrastructure for managing new clients to get them up and running quickly," Meisinger says. "We've documented everything that we do very carefully so that new employees can come in, receive clearly detailed work instructions, and then execute those job functions. And we have a supervisory staff that understands the unique issues—addiction, legal matters, child care, housing, and transportation—that these folks bring with them into the workplace. There is no such thing as a cookie-cutter program; everyone has different needs. But we can give employees the individualized support that they need to have a shot at turning their lives around."

That's exactly what Jack Dalton did for himself when he began Pioneer as a halfway house in 1962. A former attorney, Dalton had been released from prison after serving time for embezzlement. Disbarred and penniless, he had nowhere to go and nothing to lose. So he borrowed money from his friends (some of the same people whom he had stolen from) and started Pioneer, whose services grew from housing to employment. Norm Chamberlain, who had been executive director of Pioneer for 17 years, started the first work-release program in Washington State by inviting six parolees to live with him.

Larry Fehr, 47, a senior vice president who tracks the results of Pioneer's business and social efforts, says that the company's blend of a for-profit attitude toward business and a "We serve this very challenging client population that is not a warm-and-fuzzy cause," he says. "People aren't so inclined to have car washes for convicts. And so we have had to think of ways to earn money, rather than just asking people to give it to us. The ironic part, of course, is that we've done what nonprofits have forever been telling their clients to do—become more self-sufficient."

RULES FOR A TURNAROUND

Cheryl Hodges used to wake up every morning and plan how she would get the money to buy the crystal meth that she craved. How did the 41-year-old grandmother end up in such a desperate situation? After spending years raising four children and enduring a messy second divorce, Hodges decided that she'd missed out on her wild and fun-filled teenage years and made some changes to her life. A few months into her new party-all-night lifestyle, she tried methamphetamine—and got hooked. Then she started delivering the drug to earn money for her own stash. She got caught in the spring of 1997 and was sentenced to two years in prison.

Through Pioneer, Hodges was able to get into a work-release program. The new arrangement may not be as confining as prison, but it's not complete freedom either. The Department of Corrections controls her money. Hodges has a small monthly allowance; the rest goes into a savings account. She lives in the Helen B. Ratcliff House, a women's work-release facility that Pioneer owns and operates. Rooms in the facility are spartan. Hodges rises at 4 AM, waits her turn for a shower, and then wakes up her roommate so that they both will be ready when the early-morning bus arrives. Most outings are supervised, and residents can host only preapproved visitors.

At Pioneer, the rules are tough for non-work-release employees as well. Drug tests are administered regularly. Anyone who tests positive is out—period. But if employees acknowledge a problem (chemical or otherwise), then they are referred to counseling services. Only 2.4% of Pioneer workers test positive, compared with a national average of 7.3%.

The rules provide the structure that those in recovery need to take small steps forward. Still two months from the end of her sentence, Hodges is anxious about how she will fare after she is released. She knows that once the safety net of the work-release program is removed, her risk of returning to a life on drugs will increase. "My family and I are kind of nervous about it," she admits. "They see how far I've come, and they see the changes in me as a person. It would just devastate all of us if I were to relapse. But no one can say that it will never happen. It may not be what I want, but I'm scared because I'm an addict."

For those who are former offenders or recovering addicts (at least 75% of Pioneer's workforce), their ability to be open about their past mistakes makes following the rules easier. "Part of what I like about being at Pioneer is that I don't have to hide my past," says Marla Gese. "I don't flaunt it, but I don't have to hide it either.

When I first got out of prison, I applied for jobs outside of Pioneer. But I learned that if you tell the truth about your past on a traditional company's application, then nobody calls you."

For people who don't want to change, Pioneer's open and understanding environment can be the worst thing about the company. For employees who are just coasting through the system or are falling into old habits, supervisors are tough to fool. They've had personal experience with crime and addiction and are unlikely to miss the subtle signs of an addict's relapse that another employer might not immediately recognize.

Gese believes that she is a much more effective manager at Pioneer because of her own experience. "It's very easy for me to recognize many of the things that people in recovery do, such as blaming others and refusing to take responsibility," she says. "In their mind, everything is someone else's fault: 'The world owes me.' When they start in on their pitch or manipulation, I just start laughing. I say, 'Wait a minute. I've been where you are. I've probably been through more than you have. I know what you're doing. You may not recognize it, but this is what I see.'"

Not all of Pioneer's employees make it. Nearly 11% leave after 30 days. About half of those drop out on their own; the rest are asked to go. Longer-term success is more difficult to track because former employees are not obligated to stay in touch. But, thanks to a grant from the Ford Foundation, the company is trying. The results are encouraging: Based on a sample of 402 former clients, Pioneer found that 96.6% of them were still employed a year after leaving the company or completing the training.

The Pioneer route gives taxpayers a break as well. Sending an offender through a Pioneer work-release program costs $18,359 per offender annually; a traditional prison sentence costs $23,525—a figure that is misleadingly low, given that these days, Washington State prisons are at 153% capacity. Cost is certainly not an insignificant issue: Many states, including California, Maryland, and New York, now spend more on prison systems than they spend on colleges and universities. And more than 1,000 new prisons have been built in the United States since 1970.

MISSION MATTERS

It's a predictably rainy afternoon in Seattle, but Jim Ray's grin brightens the 120,000-square-foot warehouse that he supervises. Ray, Pioneer's vice president of distribution services, is beaming about a recent shipment from Hasbro. The boxes represent a big, new opportunity for work. The toy maker has 275,000 double-sided light sabers (each designed to look like the one in "Star Wars Episode I: The Phantom Menace") that are waiting to be shipped to retailers from Seattle's port. The problem is, they're defective: The engineers who designed them didn't include a protector for the battery coil in the handle. So whenever the light saber glows for more than a few minutes, the handle becomes hot. Retailers, many of which have run ads promoting the toy to whet the appetites of "Star Wars"-crazed kids, are up in arms. So Hasbro has hired Pioneer to unpack each light saber, to insert a coil protector in it, and then to repack the toy for shipment.

It is perfect entry-level work: Little training is required; the most complex part of the job is showing up on time. "We don't care where people come from," Ray says. "We want to give them a fresh start and an opportunity to take responsibility for their behavior—by showing up on time, by doing the work that's given to them, and by being cooperative. Those are the baseline skills that they're going to need in order to work anywhere else."

Ray, 49, left an impressive job as head of distribution for Starbucks to start a distribution center for Pioneer. Running the coffee company's domestic and international distribution was challenging, but Ray wanted more. His effect on Pioneer has been huge. In less than a year, the new distribution center broke even and was supplying jobs to hundreds of people, both Pioneer clients and local immigrants. "I wanted to be in an environment where I could give back," Ray explains. "Taking profits and reinvesting in people has more long-term value than being at a company that just takes from society and reaps profits. I'm a capitalist, but I'm a socially responsible capitalist."

When Ray talks about giving back, he isn't talking just about Pioneer's efforts. He sees the company not only as a business or a social service but also as a test case: If these ideas work at Pioneer, then maybe they can work everywhere. "You could go to every port city and you could do the kind of value-added distribution that we do here," Ray says. "That's the bigger picture for me: How can this become an opportunity for a community to help those who are at risk? We need to create a model here—and then duplicate it."

Ray isn't the only one who thinks that Pioneer could be a role model for other businesses. The company has several ideas for expansion, including assembling a $4.4 million venture fund with such investors as InterWest Bank, the Rockefeller Foundation, and Wells Fargo & Co., which will help Pioneer purchase businesses to add to its portfolio. Pioneer feels real pressure to grow. "Fifteen years ago, the company had revenues of $4 million," says president and CEO Burns. "Today, we have about $52 million. But we measure our worth not just in terms of dollars but also in terms of making a difference: How many more lives can we touch if we add more businesses?

"It's customary for us to invite employees to tell their stories at our annual and monthly board meetings," Burns continues. "At my first annual meeting, the woman who gave her testimonial was incredible. She brought members of the audience—including some executives from Boeing—to tears. One thing that she emphasized was the need to 'keep the company strong so that it can grow and help more people. The world needs places like Pioneer.' For us as a management team, that is exactly what it's all about."

Cheryl Dahle (cdahle@fastcompany.com) is a *Fast Company* senior writer. Contact Mike Burns (mike.burns@p-h-s.com) by email.

THE SOCIAL JUSTICE AGENDA

Pioneer Human Services is pioneering a new model for social change—and, in the process, is setting a new agenda for nonprofit organizations everywhere. In an interview with Fast Company, Pioneer president and CEO Mike Burns outlined the key points of a nonprofit agenda that emphasizes performance as well as people.

1. Untapped potential exists where you least expect it.

"Many companies evaluate workers based on only their experience and education," says Burns. "We employ some people who, at age 25 or 27, have never had a job before. They take more training, but they come up to speed and blossom incredibly quickly. We've succeeded by purposefully taking risks on people."

2. We ignore those on the margins at our peril.

"Whether you think that prison is about punishment or rehabilitation, it doesn't make sense to release people who've been locked away for years onto the streets with no job, no money, and no guidance," Burns says. "Work-release programs are a great way to help people prepare to take on responsibilities in the community. There is no evidence that crime increases when work-release programs come into a neighborhood, but we have a hard time getting sites for these programs approved."

3. If you save an individual, then you save a community.

"Once people become taxpaying, contributing citizens," says Burns, "we've helped not only them, but also their entire family. The effect is multiplied many times over. If we can reduce recidivism by chipping away at crime and drug and alcohol addictions, then we're helping reknit the social fabric."

4. Keep your charity.

"Directors of nonprofits have to realize that 'profit' is not a dirty word," Burns says. "It strengthens your organization. The nice thing about our services is that we're not looking toward every July first—the deadline for government budgets—wondering, 'Are we going to get refunded? Is the government going to eliminate this program? And if so, what do we do with our personnel?' Our programs are funded by our own resources, which gives us the freedom to base those programs on our clients' needs, not on the availability of funds."

DISCUSSION QUESTIONS FOR SECTION 3

1. What aspect(s) of Interface's environment stewardship program do you find most noteworthy?

2. The title to the second and third articles contains the words "social justice." How does the Freeplay Group attempt to meet their worthy societal objective?

3. How is Pioneer Human Services' approach similar or different from that of the Freeplay Group?

EXEMPLARY COMPANIES

This section focuses on companies that have achieved an exemplary record in the area of business ethics and social values. While all these firms have demonstrated a strong commitment to ethics, competitive challenges and the market in the 21st century have shaken them. However, leaders of these companies have indicated they will not compromise their principles despite these challenges.

The first company examined in this section is AES. As the article indicates, AES has been successful in expanding internationally during their twenty-year history. Their corporate values are: integrity, fairness, social responsibility, and fun. The "fun" value is discussed explicitly. The company's commitment to decentralization and trust has been the subject of two different Harvard Business School case studies. In addition, a *Harvard Business Review* article (January 1999) presents a long interview with Roger Sant and Dennis Bakke. In the aftermath of Enron, AES has suffered major financial reversals because they are also in the energy industry. The CEO, Dennis Bakke, has resigned, even though his honesty and commitment to corporate values remained strong. The chairman, Roger Sant, has rededicated himself to the success of the organization. (For those interested in examining AES in more detail, please see its Web site at www.aes.com.)

The second selection deals with a multinational corporation that is well known to most of us—Lego, headquartered in Denmark. The name "Lego" in Danish means "play well." The corporate values of Lego are referred to in a number of places in this selection. However, they are not completely delineated. The list of ten Lego rules is as follows: 1. Be objective and truthful. 2. Be positive and unpretentious. 3. Be economical. 4. Be international. 5. Evoke enthusiasm and inspire. 6. Encourage imagination and activity. 7. Observe characteristics. 8. Take precedence of sublimate self. 9. Always finish the job. 10. Follow company policy.

The editor visited the Billund, Denmark, headquarters and the adjacent park, Legoland, some years ago with his family. His three small boys definitely enjoyed their Lego experience. As a sign of Lego's commitment to its consumers, Lego offered families an opportunity to use Lego blocks for free to make a race car on the rainy day that we visited the park. As the article indicates, Lego has rededicated itself to a market orientation and changing with the times. It was not a nimble company in the early 1990s. However, because of its strong value system and many consumers' positive childhood experience with the product, Lego is a company that most observers hope succeeds.

The third article focuses on the London-based ad agency, St. Luke's, now six years old and flourishing. The article examines the historical context of the development of the agency by its founders. The principles upon which it is based are shown near the end of the article. This agency views its values and ethical precepts as a primary reason for its existence. The egalitarian nature of St. Luke's, as well as its innovative style and culture, set it apart from all but a few agencies anywhere in the world. As the heading "Total Role in Society" points out, St. Luke's follows the gospel of total ethics and common ownership by its employees.

The final article deals with three companies rather than one. The title of the article "Honesty is the Best Policy—Trust Us" is a signal that these firms take honesty as serious business and as a core value. One of the firms, CenterBeam, has a unique values statement, which uses quotations from famous people to emphasize each of its six core values: Customer First; Integrity; Passion; Ownership; Speed; Team; Fun (see centerbeam.com). The second company is Onset Ventures. This venture capital firm works with high-tech companies, but emphasizes keeping its word rather than worrying about short-term profits. Promise keeping is also part of its "Honesty is the Best Policy." The third firm, New Enterprise Associates, chooses teamwork over its short-term views in working to fund CenterBeam. The concluding thoughts in this article emphasize the ever-important dimension of integrity in brick and mortar, as well as Internet-based, companies.

These companies, while obviously not perfect, do set high standards for themselves. The common dimension among all six firms is that they see "financial profit" as an outcome or byproduct of their values, not as a central precept that should be followed at all costs. While some of them have suffered financial reversals and short-term setbacks, their values and ethics-based principles should ensure long-term success (defined broadly).

Power to the People

AES IS BIG, RICH—AND UNLIKE ANY COMPANY YOU'VE EVER SEEN. IT BUILDS POWER PLANTS BY HANDING POWER TO WORKERS ON THE FRONT LINES. ITS RADICAL BUSINESS MODEL HAS WORKED WONDERS IN THE UNITED STATES. CAN IT ALSO WORK IN HUNGARY, CHINA, AND BRAZIL?

Oscar Prieto had no idea how much his life was about to change. It was May 1996. Prieto, a relative newcomer to AES Corp., an independent producer of electrical power, was visiting its headquarters in Arlington, Virginia. He was meeting with a bunch of his colleagues when Thomas Tribone, a senior executive, interrupted.

"I've got fourteen people from France and some guys from Houston coming in to talk about buying a business in Rio de Janeiro," Tribone announced. "We've only got two AES people. Could one of you show up?" Prieto raised his hand and walked to a conference room down the hall. "I sat in the back and didn't pay much attention," he recalls.

The executives had gathered to discuss the privatization of Light Servicios de Electricidade (known as "Light"), one of Brazil's largest public utilities. Brazil's government had launched a massive sale of public assets. The French delegation—executives from Electricite de France (EdF), that country's giant national utility—along with representatives of Houston Light & Power, was considering a bid on the soon-to-be-auctioned Light. The group saw AES as a potential partner.

Prieto was puzzled. Why would AES be interested? His small company (which then had about 1,100 employees) was focused on the power-generation side of the business—building, buying, and operating plants, and selling the electricity from them to wholesale customers. Light was a massive public utility with more than 11,000 employees and a sprawling distribution system that served more than 2.7 million retail customers in Rio de Janeiro.

After the meeting, Tribone asked Prieto if he would like to play a lead role in this potential acquisition—a $1.7 billion deal that would cost AES about $400 million. "But Tom, we're not in the distribution business," Prieto said. "And I've never done this before."

Prieto, a chemical engineer, had worked for AES for just two years. It was his first job in the power industry: He had been hired to turn around a struggling 650-megawatt power plant in his native Argentina—the company's first joint venture in Latin America.

"You've been through a very difficult partnership," Tribone said. "You know what makes them work."

Prieto, then 43, soon left for Paris to negotiate an agreement with EdF: "I said to myself, What the hell am I doing? I'm handling such a huge, huge job all alone."

But Prieto got the job done. He moved to Rio de Janeiro and became one of Light's four directors. Then the job got really interesting. In short order, AES completed a string of deals: It signed a joint-venture agreement to buy CEMIG—an even-larger Brazilian utility, with more than 4 million customers. It broke ground on a new power plant in Uruguaiana, near Brazil's southern border. It took over the company that supplied electricity for Buenos Aires. And last October, it won a bid to distribute electricity to 800,000 customers in southern Brazil.

Today, 18 months after that fateful meeting in Arlington, Oscar Prieto works out of a 15th-floor office overlooking downtown Rio. He is a director of a major Brazilian company and a key figure in AES's rapid expansion in South America. He helicopters from one far-flung plant to another and oversees hundreds of millions of dollars in construction projects. His division has a combined customer base of 8 million homes and businesses.

"That's what happens when you raise your hand around here," Prieto says with a smile.

At most companies, Oscar Prieto's personal odyssey would be a fairy tale—far too much new responsibility, far too early in his tenure. At AES, it is standard operating procedure.

"God made us all a certain way," says Dennis Bakke, 52, AES's cofounder and CEO. "We're all creative, capable of making decisions, trustworthy, able to learn, and perhaps most important, fallible. We all want to be part of a community and to use our skills to make a difference in the world." Adds Roger Sant, 66, AES's cofounder and chairman: "If Dennis and I had to lead everything, we couldn't have grown as much as we have. People would bring deals for us to approve, and we would have a huge bottleneck. We've shifted to giving advice rather than giving approval. And we've moved ahead much faster than we would have otherwise."

Simple insights—but they have profound consequences for how AES operates. Lots of companies talk about pushing responsibility out from headquarters. Few companies push as hard or as far as AES. Just five years ago, it had fewer than 600 employees. Today it has nearly 6,000 employees (or more than 31,000, if you count those working in its joint ventures). Yet it has never established corporate departments for human resources, operations, purchasing, or legal affairs. Its headquarters staff includes fewer than 30 people.

Lots of companies talk about grassroots teams. Few companies give teams more power than AES does. A few years ago, CFO Barry Sharp estimated that the company had raised $3.5 billion to finance 10 new power plants. But, he added, he'd secured only $300 million of that sum on his own. The rest was brought in by decentralized teams. When AES raised $200 million (about $350 million) to finance a joint venture in Northern Ireland, two control-room operators led the team that raised the funds.

It sounds crazy—but it works. In 1990, the year before AES went public, the company had annual revenues of less than $200 million and profits of less than $16 million. In 1996, it had revenues of $835 million and profits of $125 million. The company opened its first plant in 1986. Today it owns or has an interest in 82 power plants, which generate nearly 22,000 megawatts of power for consumers in the United States, Argentina, China, Hungary, and other countries.

Not surprisingly, AES is a darling of Wall Street. Its 1991 public offering valued the company at $750 million. Today it has a market value of around $6 billion. Together, Bakke and Sant own about 25% of AES's shares—which translate into personal fortunes of roughly $750 million and $900 million, respectively.

But even more remarkable than the economic value that AES has created are the social values that it embraces—the ideas around which the company is built.

IF IT'S NOT FUN, DON'T DO IT

The AES mission statement declares that work should be "fun, fulfilling and exciting." But that doesn't mean Friday-afternoon beer busts. It means growth, freedom, and achievement. At AES, having fun means being challenged.

"Fun happens when you're intellectually excited," argues Sant. "It's people interacting with each other—with one idea leading to another—and getting frustrated if there isn't an answer. It's the struggle, and even the failures that go with the struggle, that make work fun."

Bakke and Sant couldn't have picked a tougher business in which to have fun. Power-plant work is hard, dangerous, and often boring. Most employees get trained in mundane, highly specialized tasks: Materials handlers move fuel to the boilers; technicians regulate fuel and temperature levels; electricians monitor and help maintain generators and other equipment.

"Specialization is the root of a lot of boredom," says Bakke. Even worse, he argues, talented specialists tend to dumb down the rest of the organization: "As soon as you have a specialist who's very good, everyone else quits thinking. The better that person is, the worse it is for the organization. Now the information goes through the specialist, so all the education flows to the person who already knows the most."

THE FRONT LINE DRIVES THE BOTTOM LINE

Bakke and Sant are idealists. They are also clear-eyed realists. They abandoned long ago an illusion to which most executives cling—that only the people at the top have the wherewithal to run the show. The best way to exercise power, the AES founders argue, is to give it up.

"The modern manager is supposed to ask his people for advice and then make a decision," says Bakke. "But at AES, each decision is made by a person and a team. Their job is to get advice from me and from anybody else they think it's necessary to get advice from. And then they make the decision."

What happens when leaders renounce their authority? Their companies become faster and more nimble. In Brazil, AES's bid for CEMIG bogged down when a joint-venture partner couldn't make up its mind. "We made our decision within days," says Alessandra Marinheiro, the AES project manager who helped fashion the bid.

"But our partner had to ask its board for approval, and that board had to ask another board. We delayed the bid—only to have the company pull out because it couldn't get final approval."

That didn't delay Marinheiro, 24, an entry-level financial analyst who became a project manager with responsibility for more than $2 billion in acquisitions—after less than a year at AES. On the day before the CEMIG auction, she lined up a new partner and reworked the bid. "We called Tom Tribone and made a decision," she recalls. "Other companies can't do that."

EVERY PERSON A BUSINESSPERSON

There's another reason why AES disperses power so widely. "If all information about finance goes to the finance department, and all information about legal matters goes to the legal department, it's impossible to get well-rounded people who can think about the whole world," Bakke says. And it's well-rounded people, he argues, who deliver extraordinary performance.

Sound fanciful? Consider the career of Scott Gardner, 29, who joined AES in 1992 right out of Dartmouth College. Gardner joined a team developing a $200 million cogeneration plant in San Francisco. "It involved a lot of work and few people to do it," he says. "I took on tasks that ranged from designing a water system to negotiating with the community to buying and selling pollution credits."

Gardner also helped lead a bid (ultimately unsuccessful) for a $225 million cogeneration plant in Vancouver, British Columbia. When a similar deal materialized in Australia, Gardner volunteered for that assignment. Two weeks later, he was on his way to Brisbane.

"My task was to understand an unfamiliar regional power system, develop a design for the plant, and prepare a financial and technical bid document—all in six weeks," he says. When Gardner's proposal made the final round of competition, his division manager had him negotiate the terms of the $75 million deal. "The stress was incredible, but I was having fun," he says.

His bid won. "I held a press conference and was interviewed by local TV stations," says Gardner, who has left AES to attend business school. "I had to pinch myself to be sure this was happening."

DON'T JUST MAKE MONEY—MAKE A DIFFERENCE

There's no denying AES's financial success. But Bakke and Sant didn't start the company so they could cash in. Bakke is a devout Christian whose ideas on business trace back to his religious beliefs. Sant is an environmentalist who has been active in organizations like the World Wildlife Fund and the Environmental Defense Fund. "This isn't about maximizing profits," Bakke insists. "We do this because it maximizes our ability to have fun and make a difference."

Of course, building and operating power plants is not one of the world's most environmentally benign endeavors. That's why AES tries to compensate for the emissions that it generates. When it built a coal-fired plant in Montville, Connecticut, it calculated that it would generate 15 million tons of carbon over 40 years. It planted 52 million trees in Guatemala—enough to offset those emissions.

As AES has moved into the developing world, its social initiatives have moved beyond environmentalism. It has funded medical care in Kazakhstan, organized food banks in Argentina, built schools in China. Roger Sant says AES started shifting gears when it built two 340-megawatt power plants in Pakistan, where the adult literacy rate is less than 40%. "You can't go to Pakistan and say that the number-one priority is global warming," he argues.

AES's practices are undeniably radical. They are also distinctly American. Decentralized authority, open-book management, challenging jobs—this is the new formula at more and more young U.S. companies. So what happens as AES goes global?

Five years ago, almost all of AES's operations were on American soil. Today, after billions of dollars worth of acquisitions and joint ventures, two-thirds of its holdings are outside the United States. AES now generates 20% of all the electricity in Hungary. It operates one of the world's largest coal-fired plants—in Kazakhstan. It has a stake in six plants in China and five in Argentina. The biggest challenge facing Bakke and Sant is whether they can do business the same way in Hungary and China as they do in Texas and Oklahoma.

Oscar Prieto's work in Brazil is a test case. Light Servicios de Electricidade, established almost a century ago, is Brazil's answer to Consolidated Edison. Founded by Canadians as a private company, Light was seized by the Brazilian government in 1979.

"That's when time stopped around here," says plant supervisor Ricardo Silva, 48, as he rides a rusty cable car to the top of a water pipeline that feeds 10 generators at Light's 600-megawatt Fontes complex. "Nothing much has happened since."

Fontes, Light's largest generating facility, is situated on a former coffee plantation in the mountains west of Rio. Until 1990, it employed more than 1,000 workers—and housed them and their families in a bucolic village built by the company. A lot has changed at Fontes since privatization. For one thing, Prieto and his colleagues have slashed the workforce by more than two-thirds. They designed a generous severance package, but there's no denying the dislocation. "A lot of people had to move away," says Silva, who has worked and lived at Fontes for almost two decades.

Such stories make Roger Sant wince. "But keeping three times as many people as you need doesn't work for anyone," he says. Adds Oscar Prieto: "The people who remain behave differently; their humor changes; their habits change. There's an inverse relation between the number of people and the quality of behavior."

That's the case at Santa Branca, a small Light facility that sits along the Paraiba do Sul river, northwest of Sao Paulo. Until AES took over Santa Branca, its only function was to redirect water to another hydrostation located down river. Yet it employed 32 full-time workers. "How many people do you need?" Prieto marvels.

Prieto chose Santa Branca as his initial experiment in transplanting AES's bottom-up culture into Light's top-heavy bureaucracy. First he announced a massive downsizing. Then he unveiled an upgrade—a $35 million construction project that will enable

Santa Branca to fuel two hydroelectric generators. Then he asked for volunteers who would run things the AES way.

He quickly picked Carlos Baldi, 34, an engineer from Fontes, to be his leader in Santa Branca. "I knew he was the right person," says Prieto. "He was young, eager to do more." Then, after agreeing on shared goals and expectations—zero accidents, thrifty construction budgets—Prieto turned Santa Branca over to Baldi.

Didn't Prieto worry about distributing too much power too fast? "I trust people—without fear or hesitation," he says. "The best way to let them perform is with absolute freedom: I release you of all constraints, including the constraints imposed by your boss."

Freedom "was very scary at the beginning," says Baldi. "Every time I had to make a decision, I thought, 'Should I call Oscar?' But he just said, 'You know better than I do—you decide.'"

Now Baldi operates the same way with his people. Claudio Jorge Coelho de Souza, 36, runs electrical-engineering projects at Santa Branca. "I'm always getting his opinion," says Baldi. Aldir Cardozo Carreiro, 47, a former maintenance supervisor, oversees the facility's entire $1.3 million operating budget. "Aldir had never done anything like this," says Baldi. "So we got him an accounting program. Now he budgets salaries, writes contracts, oversees all maintenance."

What's next for AES? According to Dennis Bakke, it involves going beyond how people work to how they're paid. Bakke has long been critical of U.S. wage-and-hour laws, which require that non-management workers be paid strictly on an hourly basis. Such laws "are one of the major hindrances to creating a fun, meaningful and empowering workplace," he wrote in a letter to then-Secretary of Labor Robert Reich in 1996.

Bakke's argument has fallen on deaf ears in the United States. So his company is introducing change in places where the barriers aren't so formidable. Plants in Argentina, Pakistan, and England are moving to an all-salary format. So are plants in South America.

Oscar Prieto experimented with the idea at Cabra Corral, Argentina, another privatized hydroelectric plant that has experienced a big downsizing. "We broke all the rules," says Prieto. "No overtime. No bosses. No time records. No shift schedules. No assigned responsibilities. No administration. And guess what? It worked!"

Now Prieto is unveiling a similar approach at Santa Branca, whose employees have punched time clocks throughout their working lives. Even for free spirits like Carlos Baldi, the new system is a shock. "Brazilians want to know exactly how much money they're going to have at the end of the month," Baldi says. "And they want to know that they're never going to have to work on Sundays."

Prieto and his colleagues know they're in uncharted territory. But they're eager to explore. "If you treat human beings fairly, they will respond as adults," he says. "It's a matter of believing in people."

Alex Markels alexm@nyct.net is a former staff reporter for the *Wall Street Journal*. He is writing a book on AES's values-driven culture.

BY CHARLES FISHMAN   FROM *FAST COMPANY* ISSUE 50, PAGE 144

Why Can't Lego Click?

THE GIANT DANISH TOYMAKER HAS A HISTORY AND A REPUTATION THAT MOST COMPANIES CAN ONLY DREAM OF. YET ITS EFFORTS TO CHANGE AND GROW WITH THE TIMES JUST WON'T CLICK.

In a land that gave birth to fairy tales and conquerors, there is a peaceful village that seems unfazed by the impatience of the modern world. For almost 70 years, the people of this village have specialized in one thing: making toys.

At first, there were only two toymakers: a carpenter and his son. Now the carpenter's grandson is the chief toymaker, and he has thousands of others working for his global company.

Lego has a history that most companies only dream about. Yet its efforts to grow with the times haven't worked out. Here's a story—a fable, really—of a noble company and its difficult encounters with a fickle, fast-moving world.

The toys that the villagers make are special, and they are known around the world. Since the days of the carpenter, each toy—from the simplest to the most elaborate—has left the workshop unfinished. To come to life, each one needs the touch and the imagination of a child.

The people of this Danish village are proud of their heritage: both the global company that they have helped create, and its impact on millions of children in faraway lands. Most of the people of the village smile through their days. But they are worried. For reasons that the toymakers haven't been able to discover, the toys they make seem to be losing their magic.

Peter Eio, who this summer retired after 20 years with Lego, remembers his first visit to Billund, the Danish village that has always been the world headquarters of Lego, and his first meeting with Godtfred Kirk Christiansen, the carpenter's son, who was then running the business. It was 1981, and Eio had just been hired to run Lego's United Kingdom operations. "I was invited to meet the owner," he says. "He asked what I noticed was different about Lego from the other firms where I'd worked."

"When I joined Lego, I'd worked for American companies my whole career. I told him that during the four interviews I had to join Lego, the word 'profit' was never mentioned," says Eio, 53. "Godtfred smiled. 'If we do all things right, the profit will come,' he said."

Godtfred died in 1995. Profits for Lego peaked the next year. In 1997, profits fell precipitously. In 1998, Lego lost almost 300 million Danish kroner before taxes. In 1999, Godtfred's son, Kjeld, laid off 1,000 people—the first big layoffs in company history. After a brief respite in 1999, Lego last year lost 1 billion Danish kroner—or roughly $120 million, on sales of about $1.1 billion. "Godtfred's philosophy worked in 1981," says Eio. "But it's a totally changed environment since then."

Lego's recent struggle is an instructive story, a fable, about an admirable company and its encounters with a fast-changing world. The lives of middle-class children have been revolutionized in the past 20 years—time compression, relentlessly programmed days, career-minded parents, electronics. Says Leah Kalboussi, head of sales for some of Lego's electronics and software products: "Kids these days are busy people."

Play itself is different today. A generation ago—with just a few TV channels, no computers, and primitive video games—children grew up in a play economy, of which entertainment was but a small, easily contained part. Today's children grow up in an entertainment economy saturated with media, in which open-ended, self-guided play is a shrinking part.

Lego's struggle is also a story about the power—and the limits—of deep-seated corporate values. It would be hard to imagine a global corporation with employees who so clearly understood their company's values, that produced more admirable products, and that had a more basic respect for its customers than Lego. But the business of engaging children has changed so much that Lego's core value, inspiring and nurturing creativity and play, doesn't seem to be helping the company succeed. If you look at what children and their parents are buying (Lego hasn't had a toy in the list of top 20 U.S. sellers any year in the past seven), it's hard not to conclude that Lego finds itself in a fight for relevance, perhaps even for survival, for which the company's 70-year history may not have prepared it.

Most companies have little relationship with their history, let alone with their core values. At Lego, the company's history is alive in the halls every day. The basic eight-stud red Lego brick was first sold in 1949, it was refined and patented in 1958, and it hasn't changed—including the recipe for the plastic used—in almost four decades. Almost every office and conference room at Lego contains a bowl of loose Lego bricks so that people can play during meetings.

Kjeld Kirk Kristiansen (his last name was accidentally misspelled with a "K" on his birth certificate) is the grandson of Ole Kirk Christiansen, the carpenter who founded Lego—and Kjeld, 54, is now CEO and the man whom employees call "the owner." The house where his father, Godtfred, grew up—a brick building with lions flanking the front steps—is now nestled amid Lego's corporate buildings. When the owner visits the group that develops toys for preschoolers, he climbs the stairs to his father's childhood bedroom.

The only thing more vivid for Lego than the bricks and the history are what are known universally within the company as "Lego values." Not just the importance of free-form play. No Lego-designed toys are allowed to portray weapons from the 20th century—although a recent exception involved a new, advanced kit for building a Sopwith Camel, the Allies' World War I biplane fighter. Long before the invention of software, Lego made all of its toys backward compatible. Bricks produced in 2001 work seamlessly with bricks from 1971. And every toy that Lego offers—even the simplest ones, given away with McDonald's Happy Meals—requires construction, the touch of a child.

You can't have a conversation of 10 minutes without staff members making an unself-conscious reference to those "Lego values." Even the small band of hip, cynical

New Yorkers posted in Lego's new SoHo office, a group busy creating online product features and a Web-based Lego community, talk about bringing Lego values to areas desperately in need of them: the Internet, games, and kids' software.

But history and values haven't helped Lego avoid turbulence. The company has been trying to find its footing for a decade. Kjeld described last year's billion-kroner loss as "disastrous." His handpicked deputy, Poul Plougmann, described the performance as "miserable." And in the wake of 2000, one of the first things that Kjeld and Plougmann did was write a "go-get-'em" booklet for employees. The cover is Lego-brick red; the title is "Remembering Why We Are Here."

For Lego—an influential, beloved company—the question is whether there is any way to adapt its history and values to the hypnotic world of Game Boy, Xbox, instant messaging, and Pokemon. Can the past be a guide to the future?

Long ago, in the Danish village, there was another time of worry. During the Depression, the carpentry business of Ole Kirk suffered greatly. The carpenter decided to focus on making things he thought nearby farmers would need to buy, even in difficult times: household goods like stepladders and ironing boards, and wooden toys like ducks, fire engines, and buses. The toys started as a sideline, but they became well known for their quality.

In 1947, Ole Kirk discovered a new material, plastic, and he brought a plastics injection-molding machine to his village—the first such machine in the entire country. Plastic toys were a strange idea, and many of Ole Kirk's toymakers were astonished and upset: "We're a wooden-toy company, Ole Kirk!"

But Ole Kirk would not be turned aside. One of his early plastic toys was a set of small building bricks that snapped together, first called "automatic binding bricks." Ole Kirk was so intrigued with them that he often carried one in his pocket.

Everyone who has ever played with Lego blocks knows the secret of their success, if only intuitively. What makes Legos work is something the company calls "clutch power." When you snap two Lego pieces together, they stay snapped. They go together with a satisfying sense of solidity, and they resist coming apart. Without adequate clutch power, you wouldn't be able to build anything complicated. It is clutch power that makes Legos such a flexible, adaptable toy. And it is that plasticity that makes playing with Legos—in the right setting—as absorbing as reading any book or playing any video game.

People who study children and how they play can't speak highly enough about these classic Lego elements. "The thing that is so compelling about Legos is their flexibility," says Lynn Galle, who is the director of the 75-year-old laboratory preschool at the University of Minnesota's well-regarded Institute of Child Development. Unlike, say, a video game, says Galle, there is no right or wrong way to play with Legos.

But anyone who hasn't looked at Lego toys since his or her own childhood is in for a rude shock. The shelves at Kmart, Target, Toys "R" Us, and Wal-Mart, aren't stocked with bins of multicolored bricks, windows, and wheels. Indeed, the blocks sometimes can be difficult to find—crowded out by a vast array of intricate Lego kits that look more like models than open-ended play toys. Whether or not there is a "correct" way to play with Legos these days, most modern Lego kits are so elaborate that they come with a folder of step-by-step construction instructions.

Ethan, an 8-year-old boy from New England, is standing in front of a huge display of Lego kits: arctic adventurers, jungle explorers, and the Lego dinosaur adventurers—a series of toys that has particularly captivated Ethan. The boy gazes longingly at the Lego Dino Research Compound—612 pieces. The box shows a Lego scientist in a Lego jeep in hot pursuit of a Lego T. Rex. It's all inside the box.

Ethan is in one of Lego's half-dozen company-run retail stores in the United States—this one in Orlando, at Downtown Disney. Ethan's grandmother comes up holding an enormous tub of Lego bricks—1,200 pieces. "With these," Grandma says, "you can do whatever you want. It gives you examples right on the front."

Grandma is funding this present. Ethan is picking. And although the dinosaur compound is $79.99, and the tub of bricks is $19.99, price isn't the point of difference. Play is. "He and I have very different ideas about Legos," says Ethan's mom, Lisa Gates, a dean at Wesleyan University, who is in Orlando on vacation. "I prefer the free-form bricks, where he can make his own universe. Ethan is most drawn to the theme-based scenarios. He has an Egyptian-pyramid-dig set and some *Star Wars* sets. He's fixated on the directions—when he builds it, he wants it to look exactly like it looks on the box. That introduces a note of anxiety into playing with Legos— did I do it right?"

The tug-of-war between Ethan's view of playing with Legos and his mother's view is a miniature of the problems that Lego itself faces—internally and in the wider world. (Ethan, for the record, goes home with the dinosaurs.) In fact, the shelves of the store in Orlando display all of the opportunity and confusion that exists in the modern world of Lego. In the beginning, there were bricks—and kids built whatever they imagined. The addition of roof tiles, windows, wheels, and trees allowed you to make more-realistic creations. Buckets of bricks are available in the store, but they attract almost no attention.

After the bricks came the themed sets—town and farm first, followed by space (almost 10 years after the moon landing), and then castle and pirate lines later. The theme sets added a dimension: You built it, the theme provided inspiration (and sometimes instruction), and you could play with what you'd built in the classic role-playing scenarios that kids dream up. The construction was less inventive, the play more so.

In 1998, Lego launched Mindstorms: programmable Lego bricks. In some ways, it was a return to the earliest roots of the company: You imagined not only what you wanted to build, but also how you wanted it to behave. You could use your computer and elegant Lego software to give your crab, your rabbit, or your robot behavior as well as a body. The heart of Mindstorms is known inside Lego as the "intelligent" brick.

At each step, the natural extension of Lego's range is encouraged by spectacular sales. Wheels are a huge hit (and today, Lego rivals Bridgestone and Goodyear to produce the most tires in the world—making upward of 175 million tires per year). When figures, or miniature people, are introduced, they are the company's biggest product. Even Mindstorms, with a starting price of $199, exceed expectations.

In 1999 came the biggest gamble of all: In partnership with Lucasfilm Ltd., Lego launched 14 *Star Wars*-themed kits. Here, Lego added a new facet to Lego play: storytelling. It was still Lego, but it was *Star Wars* Lego. The kits assembled into recognizable *Star Wars* vehicles, scenes, and characters. Kids knew the story that they were buying a kit for; the toy came not just with a design, but with a plot as well. The *Star Wars* products were the biggest sellers in company history.

It was Godtfred Kirk Christiansen (GKC, as he was known) who focused his father's company on the "automatic binding bricks," who imagined a whole system of play built around them. And it was GKC who institutionalized the value of free-form play. Each innovation tested that value.

The early space-themed sets caused some worry—space was not "real" play. Kids had experience with towns and farms, but what did they know of space? Plenty, it turned out.

Adding directions was not done lightly—how free-form could the building be if it required directions? But increasing the building challenges meant providing basic instructions.

The stories of two recent products, though, really show how Lego is struggling to figure out, and adapt to, the changed world of children. When Peter Eio, the recently retired head of Lego's operations in the Americas, started thinking about a collaboration between Lego and *Star Wars*, it was late 1997. In some ways, Lego had already let the modern toy world evolve around it. In the United States, the largest toy market in the world, almost half of all toys are licensed products—from *Sesame Street* stuffed animals to *Baywatch* Barbie.

But Lego in the late 1990s was totally self-sufficient. It produced no licensed toys—and never had. When Eio, worried about missing out on licensing, started to cast about for a partner, what was he looking for? "A company that reflected the same corporate and educational values we had," he says. The natural choice: Lucasfilm, keeper of the *Star Wars* products. Executives at Lucas, it turned out, had wanted to partner with Lego for a long time, according to Howard Roffman, president of Lucas Licensing Ltd. So when Eio and a small team approached Roffman, they found an eager audience.

Executives in Billund couldn't have been more horrified. Says Eio: "The initial reaction was, 'You guys are crazy.'" It wasn't the Lego way. "We had been such a purist company," Eio says. "We tended to want to do everything within ourselves." Even the computerized Lego pieces are produced at Lego factories.

The debate over whether to do *Star Wars* products took place among Lego's dozen most-senior executives over the course of six months. One board member at the time said to Eio, "Over my dead body will you be launching *Star Wars* in Europe."

In the end, says Eio, the only reason the Lego *Star Wars* products were produced was that the owner, Kjeld, decided they would be. The *Star Wars* products were "a blockbuster, worldwide," says Eio. "It was the biggest product launch in history." The lesson went beyond the value of licensing. What kids were buying was something that Lego had never offered: a story. Says Eio: "It led us to say, Storytelling is important."

Star Wars has paved the way for a product that in some ways is the least Lego-like ever—something that even Kjeld Kirk Kristiansen says has a "different" look. "Parents may not identify it immediately as Lego," he says. "But kids will."

The new product line is a world of action figures known as Bionicle. The line includes six hulking heroes, six dwarflike wise ones, and five technovillains. They inhabit a tropical island called Mata Nui. Each category of Bionicle has a name (Toa, Turaga, Rahi), each individual creature has a name (Pohatu, Kopaka, Onua), and the geography of Mata Nui is carefully imagined—right down to the creation of a new system of measurements exclusive to the world of Bionicle. The creatures look like the kinds of robots that an 11-year-old boy would draw on his math notebook during a tedious lesson in fractions.

The Bionicle series of toys—introduced this spring in Europe, this summer in the United States—is radical in any number of ways for Lego. But the most important departure is that none of the figures have a "play meaning" independent of their story: the legend of Mata Nui. You can buy one and build it—but when you're done, unless you know the story, you won't have a clue as to what you've got.

Lego invented the Bionicle creatures, and a Lego product-development team wrote the legend of Mata Nui. Lego even invented the word "bionicle"—a combination of biological and chronicle. Here then is a Lego product (the intricate creatures need to be assembled; the most elaborate have hundreds of pieces) that is in some ways the opposite of the basic brick. On its own, it has no appeal. Only the story invests Bionicle with fun—and Lego made up the story as well as the creatures. What Lego does not provide is a resolution in the battle between the liberating Toa heroes and the deadly Makuta villains.

Lego is hoping that Bionicle will be a hit on the scale of *Star Wars*. The Toa, the heroic Bionicle toys, wear masks—kids can collect 72 different "masks of power and knowledge." Each mask has a name as well. Can you say, "Pokemon"?

The toymakers in the village know as well as anyone that childhood is often a reflection of the grown-up world around it. Sad as it made some of the toymakers to think about, their toys had not kept up with kids. The plastic Lego pieces were beautiful and fun. But what if Ole Kirk had shrugged and said, "Sure, you are right. We are a wooden-toy company. Forget plastic"?

Admitting that childhood has changed—and perhaps that the toys haven't changed enough to keep up—isn't an answer to the problems, of course. It is simply the question itself. Chief toymaker Kjeld Kirk Kristiansen has many experts, designers, and advisers to help him make sense of the new world of children, to make sense of the modern child, to find ways to recapture the magic. What ultimately rescues the chief toymaker, though, is a visit from the ghost of his grandfather, Ole Kirk. "Childhood has changed," Ole Kirk says. "Children have not."

The original Legoland theme park in Billund sits adjacent to company headquarters. The thing that is instantly striking is the size of the place: Everything is scaled to children. There are even child-sized toilets. In the Legoland Hotel, there are huge cushions in the shape of Lego blocks—and kids use them to make forts and clubhouses, right in the public spaces of the hotel. No one discourages them. Among dozens of randomly selected Lego employees from three countries, not one said a single unkind or snide word about children. Nor was there a sense within Lego that today's children are baffling or mysterious, let alone bratty or overindulged.

The people of Lego trust children. The company's slogans include lines like, "Children are our role models" and "We believe in nurturing the child in every one of us." To an outsider, sayings like that might seem cheesy. In the context of Lego's culture, though, they are part of a fundamental respect for children that is often hard for even loving parents to sustain. That appreciation for the minds of children is as important a corporate asset as the eight-stud red brick itself.

But it doesn't exempt Lego from the discipline of the market. And Lego has made a lot of mistakes in the past 20 years—the biggest of which was confusing growth with success. The decade of the eighties was a period of dramatic expansion for Lego. Because the company is privately held, it releases limited financial data. But consider this: From its founding in 1932 until 1978, sales reached roughly 1 billion Danish kroner (about $112 million by today's exchange rates). In just the next 10 years, the slope of the sales chart rocketed upward, increasing five-fold, from 1 billion kroner in 1978 to 5 billion kroner in 1988.

The growth made Lego look great—but through the 1980s, while VCRs, video games, cable TV, and computers cascaded in on kids, Lego was really just expanding its sales to its target market around the world. The explosion in sales represented not an explosion in innovative products but the company's (previously slow-going) globalization really taking hold. In the 1990s, with Lego available to kids from Israel to Korea, the sales curve flattened. Between 1988 and 1998, sales did not even double.

In fact, Lego had become a slow company—if not smug, then complacent. Lego formed a partnership with MIT in 1984, and it endowed a professorship in the MIT Media Lab in 1989—but it didn't produce the "intelligent brick" until 1998. Despite the popularity of the programmable brick, Lego has been unable to bring the price down and turn it into a mass-market product.

Kjeld Kirk Kristiansen realized that Lego needed to change course in the early 1990s. "We became a heavy institution," says Kristiansen. "We were losing our dynamism—and our fun also. It has taken 10 years to get things back on track."

Given the astonishing size of last year's losses, it's not clear whether things are back on track. Kristiansen is a mild-mannered man: He smokes a pipe, has the reflective manner to go with it, and has a strong will when he wants to—he backed not only the *Star Wars* deal, but also Mindstorms and Bionicle. Kristiansen must juggle a three-part legacy that often seems to pull Lego in conflicting directions. His father, GKC, handed over a well-managed company poised at the edge of global scale—a vision that Kjeld has been able to realize. But GKC also handed over a company that had become conservative—so conservative that even as it grew, it lost touch with its audience.

The core legacy of Lego remains a toy, the basic brick, with almost universal appeal. That toy represents an important set of values about free-form, imaginative play. An association of British toy retailers, and both *Fortune* and *Forbes* magazines, named Lego the toy of the 20th century. The problem is that in this century, the brick may no longer be an effective way of inspiring that kind of play in kids older than 6 or 7.

And then there is the legacy of Kjeld's granddad, Ole Kirk Christiansen. Ole Kirk, it turns out, was the real family radical. He bought a molding machine to make plastic toys in 1947. By way of comparison, another famous plastic product made its debut just the year before: Tupperware.

Lego today is as much the result of Ole Kirk's daring as of GKC's prudence. Ole Kirk was the innovator; he set the bar for quality, and Lego has never fallen short of it. (Have you ever seen a broken Lego piece?) GKC is the one who really invested Lego with what people now think of as the company's core play values: encouraging imagination and putting the child in charge.

Kjeld tells a story about his dad: "In 1983, someone came to him and showed him video games. It was the first time he had seen electronic toys, the first game consoles. He refused to do anything with it. He was very true to the core." Well, yes and no. Can you imagine the reaction of Ole Kirk to video games? It wouldn't have taken him 15 years to produce cool Lego video games—games that, as it turns out, do translate Lego values from the tactile to the virtual world.

Lego has changed in just the past five years. Product cycle times are falling: In time for Father's Day this year, Lego Direct, the catalog and Internet-sales division, produced the Sopwith Camel biplane kit. The plane was designed in a single day, and the kit was approved in something like two weeks. Lego has gotten religion on licensed toys completely—perhaps too completely. Its preschool line includes Winnie the Pooh Lego sets and Bob the Builder Lego sets—and the company this fall will roll out extremely secret, extremely elaborate Harry Potter Lego sets.

Lego is also discovering an important aspect of storytelling: the creation of ongoing Lego characters with whom kids can identify. Beyond Bionicle, a new adventurer named Jack Stone is being aimed at younger kids. And Lego, which has often seemed to float great products onto store shelves and then wait to see if anyone notices them, is cautiously trying some modern, even viral, marketing techniques.

Kjeld is trying to remix the culture of Ole Kirk and the culture of GKC. His dad, Kjeld says, would have thought Bionicle was "going too far. But it is a good example of expressing our values in a cool, contemporary way."

"Lego values are not just in the brick," Kjeld continues. "They are in what you get out of the brick." Lego the company needs to learn to be more like its core product, Lego the brick: nimble, adaptable, plastic—but fundamentally unchanged—no matter what kind of creation it is a part of.

To be both fair and blunt, Lego has had only two daring, visionary moments: One came from Ole Kirk's insistence on plastic toys and the future of the brick. The other came from GKC's insistence that a whole system of play could be built around the brick. The most recent of these two moments is 40 years gone. It is time for Kjeld and his team to find a similar leap. Lego can survive a long time by making good products. But trendiness—even high-quality trendiness like Bionicle and Harry Potter—is not leadership. Once, for a brief moment, Lego changed the way kids played as well as the way kids learned to think. Lego hasn't been that kind of leader in a long time.

Kjeld's chief deputy, Poul Plougmann, a former VP of finance at Bang & Olufsen, sounds almost like a member of the family when he talks about Lego. The company, he points out, has a much larger presence than its business would justify. A billion-dollar-a-year business, in global terms, is tiny. But according to research that Lego follows closely, the Lego brand is the seventh most powerful worldwide among families with children, behind only such names as Coca-Cola and Disney. People take Lego seriously, which is good news; but that view has created a legacy of expectations not to be trifled with.

Plougmann explains the value of Bionicle, for instance, by way of metaphor. Many kids, by the time they are 11 or 12, no longer think Lego is cool. They've moved on to action figures, war games, video games. Plougmann describes those kids as out on a frozen lake, in need of rescue. Bionicle is a way for them to step back off that ice. "We offer them a ladder across the ice," he says. "Bionicle is a craze. It's cool. It's a great story." His eyes twinkle. "It's a recruiting tool. We need to take those kids back.

"The important thing," says Plougmann, "is that we not grow beyond our values. We are here only to develop kids. And we should be smart enough to make a business out of it."

Charles Fishman (cnfish@mindspring.com), a senior editor at *Fast Company,* spent many hours playing with Legos—both as a 9-year-old and again for this story. Visit Lego (http://www.lego.com), or learn about the legend of Mata Nui (http://www.bionicle.com), on the Web.

The Ad Agency to End All Ad Agencies

ST. LUKE'S, A REBELLIOUS YOUNG AGENCY SPUN OUT OF THE ONCE-REVOLUTIONARY CHIAT/DAY, PRACTICES WHAT IT PREACHES—THE GOSPEL OF TOTAL ETHICS AND COMMON OWNERSHIP.

It's lunchtime at St. Luke's, a one-year-old advertising agency on the edge of London's Bloomsbury district, and the daily battle for Ping-Pong supremacy has resumed in the corporate lunchroom. Today's employee-competitors are not Andy Smith and Vince Gant; true to the British fondness for nicknames they are "Smudger" and "Banco." Because the two contestants are more adept at graphic production and finance than Ping-Pong, a lob occasionally lands solidly, if unintentionally, in someone's plate of pasta. On a nearby shelf a boombox blasting Tchaikovskys "1812 Overture" sounds an appropriate anthem for this agency's explosively original experiment in ownership structure, management, and business philosophy.

Smudger and Banco, as well as all of the diners—every single one of the 55 employees of St. Luke's—own the company. Not the token percentage that accompanies the traditional corporate stock participation program—they own it all. Everyone holds equal shares—from the people who answer the switchboard to the creative director. St. Luke's was created with an obscure communal ownership structure, established by the British "Qualifying Employee Shareholder Trust." The acronym has a heroic ring: it is referred to as a QUEST.

A five-member council governs the firm. Rather than call itself a "Board"—which smacked too much of pinstripes and privilege – the group borrowed the acronym to call itself the Quest. Two seats on the Quest are elected by the employees; they are now occupied by a print production manager and an account executive, positions that at any other ad agency would be decidedly low in the management food chain. All financial decisions are debated publicly and voted on by a treasury committee made up of everyone in the company who commits money on behalf of the agency or its clients.

But the Quest is more than a name for the firm's ownership structure and governing council. It also fits the sense of mission that infuses the work of the men and women of St. Luke's, who see themselves on a larger quest to offer a profoundly different model of what the advertising industry must become: honest, ethical advertising that represents a company's Total Role in Society. Advertising, in short, that takes the advertising out of advertising.

In case anyone needs a reminder about this corporate mission, placards in the company's hallways proclaim St. Luke's crusade:

Profit Is Like Health.
You Need It, But It Is Not What You Live For.
The Treasury Monitors the Profit We Need.
The Quest Monitors the Lives We Lead.

The sentiments seem vaguely Orwellian, mildly messianic, and absolutely alien. But it is part of St. Luke's distinctive heritage: this agency is a revolutionary child of Chiat/Day, in its time the most revolutionary of ad agencies. In fact, St. Luke's was born at the moment that Chiat/Day ceased to exist as an independent, questing firm.

Now the young agency has picked up the torch, seeking to redefine what advertising is and how it works. The implications, according to the people at St. Luke's, go beyond advertising to the heart and soul of business.

It is an industry of alchemists.

Copywriters and art directors routinely use the sorcery of slogans and images to turn toothpaste into a sexual lure, athletic shoes into a totem of hipness, and gasoline into an expression of manliness. Yet despite its ability to transmute the industry has been stuck with a decidedly leaden image of its own. A 1995 Gallup poll asked Americans to rank more than two-dozen occupations in terms of honesty and ethics. Advertising executives were narrowly defeated for last place by members of Congress and used-car salesmen.

The code of St. Luke's, in contrast to this pervasive image, is positively chivalrous. Andy Law, the firm's chairman, is a vicar's son with a degree in Greek and Latin literature. He has been known to interrupt a discussion of a client's marketing problem with a tangential anecdote of how the hexameter meter of Homer's "Iliad" approximates the sound of hoofbeats approaching Troy.

Sitting at a table on the perimeter of the St. Luke's "refectory" (the company cafeteria for those working on the other side of the Atlantic), Law sweeps an upraised palm over the room as if consecrating the diners. "I'm just working with the raw material I have," he claims, as he explains the genesis of St. Luke's. "These people were all teenagers when Thatcher came to power. These people were adolescents when AIDS reared its head. Their interests are self-motivation, personal growth, and working for a company they're proud of."

About a year ago, "these people" also worked at another ad agency, one with its own reputation for eccentricity. That's because in a previous incarnation St. Luke's was the London office of Chiat/Day.

This lineage is instructive. During their orbit as the London satellite of the wildly gyrating planet known as Chiat/Day, the people who would eventually form St. Luke's acquired their penchant for antithesis and their taste for risk. And it is ultimately the decay of Chiat/Day's gravitational field which triggered the birth of this unique new agency, for St. Luke's is fashioned from fragments rescued from a culture in collapse.

In the New Testament, the third book, the gospel of Luke, tells the parable of the son who wastes his wealth through riotous living. In the history of this St. Luke's, the story is reversed; here it is the prodigality of the parent on which the allegory spins.

Founded in 1968 by Jay Chiat and Guy Day, Chiat/Day flourished for decades as an agency marked by equal parts creativity and arrogance. In the early 1990s its billings reached $1.1 billion; Advertising Age called Chiat/Day the "Agency of the Decade." By 1992, Chiat/Day had become one of the most famous—and infamous brand-names in the advertising business. It created perhaps the most recognized commercial of all time—the Apple Super Bowl-halftime "1984" ad—and launched the Energizer bunny. Its quirky creative work in the 1980s for Nike, Reebok, and other big name clients earned it a cult-like status within the industry.

Chiat/Days provocative work for its clients was matched by its frequent reinvention of itself. Long before the concept of the open-plan office had become popular, chairman Jay Chiat had demolished office doors in order to shatter hierarchies. Later, boasting that he had stripped employees "of all their ego needs," he banished desks entirely and implemented one of the country's first "virtual offices." The company's quixotic culture bred a pious devotion among Chiat/Day's employees. A company T-shirt proclaimed the revolutionary corporate creed: "We're the pirates, not the navy."

By the early 1990s, Jay Chiat had become convinced that the ad industry was an elephant lumbering toward its graveyard. The process of producing advertising had become convoluted, requiring a huge support staff, which Chiat saw as extraneous, even detrimental, to the creative process.

In 1992, with characteristic fanfare, Chiat announced his intention to create "The Agency of the Future." In 1992 he assembled a hand-picked team representing each of the agency's core disciplines and asked them to figure out where the advertising industry was going and what Chiat/Day needed to do to get there first. From the London office Andy Law and David Abraham, an account director, were brought in to participate.

From the beginning the omens were dark.

On May 3, 1992, the members flew into Los Angeles for their first meeting—only to find the city in flames. A full-scale riot had erupted in the wake of the Rodney King verdict; the entire city was on alert, braced for much worse. Whisked off to the Ritz-Carlton in Laguna Niguel for three days of meetings, the group began its work, dubbed itself "The Chrysalis Committee" as a sign of regeneration, and sought to invent the future.

Getting to work, the Chrysalis group focused nervously on the micro-issues that most agency's grapple with. Should Chiat/Day spin its media department off as separate unit? How should the agency approach the Net and its impacts on the communication stream between clients and customers? How could the agency get paid to do more strategic thinking—which is fun—and less execution—which isn't?

Over a series of meetings that stretched into the next year, the Chrysalis committee began to suspect the real crisis facing Chiat/Day—and the entire corporate world—was that there was something wrong with business itself. Something systemic.

One afternoon, Law and Abraham walked into a Chrysalis meeting, propped up a picture of Aristotle on an easel and drew a single word on the chalkboard:

"It's a Greek word," Law told the group. "It means 'ethics.' And we think this is what we've been looking for."

Law and Abraham proposed that Chiat/Day, which had successfully managed to eliminate doors and desks, had one more anachronism it needed to dispose of: advertising. If the engine of 20th-century economic growth had been marketing, they argued, the successful companies of the 21st century would prosper through the willful application of a set of principles first described 2,500 years ago by Aristotle: ethics.

In an increasingly balkanized world of communications, a corporation's interaction with its stakeholders ultimately would become its most powerful communications medium. Ethics would not be an option, but a requirement.

In the Chrysalis groups imagined narrative, Chiat/Day would become a strategic consultancy helping clients understand and design their "TRS"—their Total Role in Society. To Chiat, the appeal of graduating from merely communicating a client's ethos to designing it was irresistible. He decided to move the Chrysalis group from the philosophical to the practical by joining the committee himself.

His membership lasted three hours.

With an impatient Chiat sitting at one end of the conference room table, the group timidly identified a company whose TRS was in need of repair: Chiat/Day. The employees were worn out and the creative work had long ago become pedestrian. There was widespread lack of employee faith in a stock participation program which had tilted huge blocks of shares toward the agency's top management. Before presuming to articulate and fix a clients Total Role in Society, the group suggested, Chiat/Day needed to heal its own.

This was not a diagnosis Jay Chiat wanted to hear. As famous for his temper as for his vision, Chiat went ballistic, grabbing his coat and storming from the room. The Agency of the Future was history. As far as its life at Chiat/Day was concerned, Chrysalis would never get past the larval stage.

While the task force had been musing over the future, the agency's board of directors had been confronting the firm's past. Queasy with debt from a failed acquisition binge, Chiat/Day faced massive repayments. There was only one way for the board simultaneously to relieve the debt and realize the value of the stock they had all amassed. A show of hands sealed the agency's fate.

In January1995, Omnicom, the communications conglomerate, announced that it would buy Chiat/Day and merge the rebel with TBWA, a larger agency with a reputation for dependable, if somewhat stolid, work.

As for Chiat/Day, the pirates were exhausted. After a voyage of 25 years, it was time to join the navy.

News that they were to be merged with TBWA flared like a backdraft through the halls of the London office of Chiat/Day. To employees who had been indoctrinated in the belief that they were creatively superior, the thought of marriage with the stodgy TBWA was repellent. Called for a comment by "Campaign," the industry's weekly trade magazine, Andy Law publicly announced that he had no intention of being eaten by the omnivorous Omnicom.

A hasty peace conference was arranged with the owners-to-be, who were anxious for the acquisition to proceed without any public signs of discord.

Law was convinced that a merger with TBWA would effectively mean spiritual death for his employees. "I knew we'd all end up in the basement of TBWA," said Law. He returned from the meeting with Omnicom and drew a line across a small corner of the office.

"I'm leaving," he told the others in the London office. "I don't want to unduly influence you, so I'm going to work over here and you can decide what you want to do." After a stunned silence, first one, then another, and finally all the employees crossed the line to Laws side. It was a mutiny—the pirates were still afloat.

Law made calls that night to all his clients. None particularly cared who owned the company, as long as the quality of the work didn't suffer. With the employees and clients behind him, Law called Omnicom and told them there would be no merger with TBWA as far as London was concerned. "You have nothing over here," Law told TBWA President Bill Tragos, "Nothing."

Tragos was furious. But Omnicom soon realized there was only one public position that would calm stockholders and the hungry trade press: the sale of the London office of Chiat/Day to Law and his associates. A deal was struck. A seven-year payback based on a percentage of profits—plus one U.S. dollar.

Andy Law had bought himself an ad agency.

Within a matter of weeks, he gave it away.

Once the adrenaline from the mutiny had subsided, Law and Abraham realized they now had sole responsibility for the paychecks of their fellow employees. They were no longer the London office of a multinational mothership—they were just one more tiny, independent ad agency in one of advertising's toughest towns.

Since all the employees had joined in the decision to jump ship, Law felt they should all have a voice in the design of the new vessel. They locked the doors of the agency, and the entire company sequestered itself for three days to invent their own future. Law sat back and listened as the group spoke of the corporation not as a disembodied third-person, but as a container for their own personal values. They wanted to go beyond the boosterism of the typical corporate mission statement with its call for "team structures" and "flat hierarchies." They wanted a concrete mechanism for universal commitment and contribution—and they wanted it deeply and permanently imbedded into the structure of the company.

To Law and Abraham, the lament sounded familiar. It echoed the issues with which they had struggled on the Chrysalis committee—and once again, it appeared as if Aristotle and his ethics might provide a solution.

"There will be the same equality between the shares as between the persons," Aristotle had observed in his commentaries on what he called "distributive justice." Law now took those words, not as a definition, but as a command. Chiat/Days culture had been dissolved by the world's most effective solvent: money. Law was determined not to make the same mistake. He asked the company's attorneys to devise a corporate structure that would divide the ownership of the new company equally among its employees.

St. Luke's is owned by a trust, and its affairs governed by a five-member council. By law, one trustee must be an outside attorney; the other four trustees are divided equally between representatives of the firm's senior managers and it's "rank-and-file" employees. To fill their two slots, the employees hold an election.

On the day St. Luke's was founded, 25% of the trust's shares were distributed equally among the employees. Those who leave must sell their shares back to the trust. The government forgives any gain in share value as long as the proceeds are used to make a major capital investment such as a house or car. But employees need not leave to realize the value of their shares. They may sell part, but not all, of their shares at any time—a guarantee that all employees are always stockholders.

St. Luke's is revalued every year, along with its share price, and a new block of shares is awarded, again equally, to all employees. So, for example, a new creative superstar who joins St. Luke's will be awarded shares—but will have fewer shares than a receptionist who's been with the agency since the beginning. "That's the way we get rid of ego and greed," says Law.

Visitors entering St. Luke's have the tendency to gape with the slack-jaws of pilgrims—this is a company where the physical design matches the philosophy. For openers, the company has no desks. Employees have traded personal workspaces for "brand rooms," large client-specific, glass-enclosed conference rooms where the team for that account meets, generates ideas, and stores work-in-progress. Between meetings and visits to clients, employees take a seat at any one of dozens of computers that they share communally.

"You should see the young people come and visit the company," says David Abraham. "You can see in their eyes this feeling of, 'God.' This isn't utopia, but we've taken away a lot of the things that are wrong about agencies, a lot of the emperors new clothes."

St. Luke's, just one year old, generates annual billings of 45 million pounds ($72 million). It's the fasted growing agency in London, meeting its 1996 revenue target in just the first for months. Clients include the Midland Bank, BBC One Radio, and a line of cosmetics for Boots, a chain of drugstores. Last spring, Ikea awarded its U.K. account to St. Luke's, as did Eurostar, the struggling English Channel rail system.

The walls and shelves of most agencies are abundantly bric-a-bracked with the trophies they've bagged at industry award shows. St. Luke's wins no contests—for the simple, stubborn reason that the agency refuses to enter any.

Law points to what he considers to be a more convincing expression of industry acclamation: envy. A recent "Impact" magazine poll asked London's art directors and copywriters where they would most like to work. Tiny St. Luke's took third position.

Four blocks south of St. Luke's, a sign in the greasy window of a hotel café peddles "Virginia Woolf Burgers." A plaque hovering above a nearby sandwich shop directs eyes to a garret which once sheltered Yeats. A mansion was Keynes's, an office was Eliot's. This is Bloomsbury, ground-zero in the post-Victorian revolt in literature, painting, and morality. The real estate here continues to stimulate dissent.

"We've turned our backs on the advertising village," says Andy Law. The "village," specifically, is the London advertising community, which appears to be equally keen on ignoring St. Luke's.

"The other agencies in town paid attention for about one nanosecond," says Isabel Bird, whose team-building consultancy, The Coaching House, works with many of London's most senior ad executives. "They thought the name sounded silly, like a hospital."

But Bird also senses a deep unease within the industry. "Every single agency I've been to is looking for a new process, because people are dead. They all kind of grab bits of money and success hurls them back. The fun isn't there any more. The Saatchis are calling it 'Dare to Be Different, Creativity in Everything We Do, Every Single Department Has To Be Creative.' Leo Burnett is saying, 'Were in the Idea Business— Everybody's Going to Be Coming Up With Ideas.' It's the same thing. Every agency is talking about process. And how 'our process should be creative.' St. Luke's is doing it."

To Andy Law and David Abraham, their efforts are a general restorative for business as a whole. They evangelize the power of ethics in business, a message they first articulated on the Chrysalis committee and which they have now instantiated in their own company.

"Everyone will think differently about the planet in the year 2000," says Abraham, "and suddenly a lot of pennies will drop and a lot of opinions and political climates will change and a lot more thinking will have been done about business and society generally. Well no longer be seen as all that revolutionary."

An open window in the St. Luke's library leads to a narrow patch of tar-papered terrace. A few of the employees have crawled through the narrow opening and onto the roof to enjoy a moment of sunshine on what feels like the first Spring day.

"We can keep explaining it," says David Abraham as he looks out over the London rooftops, "but this is just us, this is the company we are, this is the company we want to run, this is what we want to do."

Stevan Alburty (alburty@earthlink.net) is a freelance writer based in New York City and former MIS director for Chiat/Day.

THE LAW OF ST. LUKE'S

Chairman Andy Law's Observations on the Future of Advertising.

Cultural Resonance

Our goal is to produce communications that bear no resemblance to any advertising genre. Advertising is an artifact outside of real life; what we produce becomes part of everyday life itself. We're looking for cultural resonance. For example, we produced a piece of work for Ikea, the large furniture retailer, that's actually a protest song: women protesting having to have chintz in their homes. We're encouraging them to chuck it out. Now this campaign has entered everyday life—it's in politics, it's in all the papers, it's on television. People are talking about it because it taps into what's going on right now.

We don't even call ourselves an advertising agency. We call ourselves a communications resource office. The truth about companies has more energy than any fabricated advertising slogans. Every company has its own truths. It's even more true on the Net, a modern version of the old marketplace. There will still be people bullshitting on it, but the people who are putting honest communication across will succeed.

Inventive Early

We use a process that we call "get inventive early." It sounds long, but it's actually faster than the normal process. There are fewer mistakes and the client is part of the team.

We start by gathering everyone around the table as equals, and they think in free-form about the problem they've been given. There's no rule about who's got the greatest ability to contribute. The idea is king. Rather than having one person whose job is to write the creative brief for a project, we have a creative feeding frenzy among the whole group.

Then about a week later we have a strategic work session. We get the client in to combine its knowledge of the market with our creative input. We tell the client, "We're not magicians here. We want to know what you know. You may not even know what it is you know. So we're going to get it out of your heads." Together we write the brief.

Two weeks after that, we have a creative work session. We have a room with hundreds of pieces of paper, or bits of film, or photographs—all sorts of things that are the project team's first thoughts. The client comes into the room, and we say, "Nothing's for sale. Don't tell us what you like or don't like." What we want to discuss is the most culturally resonant idea. Only then do we return with something that we think will work.

Ego and Greed

The only thing that changes people's lives is when you change the fundamental structure of ownership. Most advertising agencies are groups of entrepreneurial, self-employed people who get together to make

THE LAW OF ST. LUKE'S (CONTINUED)

themselves a million bucks. But if you create an agency designed to make you rich, the same thing always happens. You put all your energy into years one, two, and three. By year four you've got lots of people working for you. Then they start having a few ideas themselves and asking for option schemes and shares. By years five and six you're already thinking how to get your money out, and in years seven and eight, you sell the company. It's the most uncreative form of business you can imagine—you destroy the thing you created in order to make it successful for you.

We've created this company to live beyond us. We're just renting resources. Remember that we're a collective here—everybody is.equal. What's disappeared are ego and greed, the two major driving forces behind the advertising business.

Tough Utopia

Our challenge is, How do we maintain this culture as we get bigger? Every October 18, we go away and reinvent the company for the people who are in it that day—not for the people in the past. This isn't a company that lives on the great heroic deeds of how we went to Madison Avenue and bought the company. That's irrelevant. What's relevant are the people in it today, their ambitions for it, and how they can make it work.

A lot of people say this is Utopia. It is a different way of working, but it's not some kind of hippie, freeloading operation. For example, we have two reviews a year. And the reviews are tough. Before we hire new people, each department head has to decide if they need another person. They then find a series of candidates who have to be interviewed by at least four other people from other departments. It's very time-consuming. But if you're going to give away a piece of the company to somebody, you want to make sure you get the right person.

And our advertising has to work. Our clients are tough. They're big businesses here; we don't have any small clients. So the advertising has to work—and it does. It's more resonant. It goes further and deeper in the way it communicates.

Total Role in Society—A Primer

The Chrysalis committee never filed a formal report. But its members generated a variety of interim documents, thinking papers, and drafts. The following excerpts, adapted from materials prepared by David Abraham and Consultant Susan Link, reflect the committee's efforts to frame the idea of a company's Total Role in Society (TRS).

Ten Principles of TRS

1. It is the potential of all business to benefit society. The maximization of that benefit will be a company's primary marketing differentiation in the 21st century.

THE LAW OF ST. LUKE'S (CONTINUED)

2. In the future, a company will have to be a trusted social citizen before it can sell or advertise effectively.

3. In the next century, the essential selling point of a company will be its Total Role in Society TRS is an evaluation of an organization among the totality of its stakeholders.

4. TRS reflects the principle that the maximization of profits is the requirement of business, but not its purpose.

5. The persuasiveness of any message relies upon the quality of its reception among all of its stakeholders: Shareholders, employees, clients, vendors, customers, competitors, the local community, the environment, families of employees, consumer groups, the legislature.

6. Companies that are seen and believed to be delivering positive contribution to those they touch will be rewarded economically and encouraged to continue.

7. A company can better maximize its profits if it sells or advertises its products or services as part of an integrated TRS strategy that holistically and honestly embraces all of its constituents.

8. There is a law of reciprocity between communicator and recipient. The recipient must be rewarded, not just spoken to with qualities integral to the communication itself.

9. The greatest barrier to a corporation's success is a misalignment of intent and behavior.

10. Communications are a magnifier. Advertising and public relations no longer control perceptions, they are lenses that magnify alignment as well as misalignment.

Four Steps to Achieving TRS

1. Qualitative audit of a company's mission, operations, products, services, and communications: Who are your stakeholders and what do they need? What is your company's perceived company reputation? What is your company's ideal company reputation?

2. Strategic evaluation: What can your company deliver from its core competency to society that will enhance your company's reputation and maximize its value? ("I'm IBM and I'll make the planet smarter.") What current activities are in line with this TRS? ("I'm Delta and I banned smoking on all worldwide flights.") What current activities are not in line with this TRS? ("I'm Reebok and kids kill each other for my shoes.")

3. Design Creative development of communications, programs, and policies that aggressively enrich a company's relationship with all of its stakeholders.

4. Implementations: Instead of merely communicating your values within the organization, how can you actually enroll everyone on its ideation? (Self-generated persuasion.)

Honesty Is the Best Policy— Trust Us

THESE SILICON VALLEY LEADERS ARE TAKING THE ETHICAL HIGH ROAD—AND BETTING THAT IT'S THE ROAD TO SUCCESS.

It's always fascinating to step inside a Silicon Valley start up and ask the people there to share stories about what makes their company special. The anecdotes that rank-and-file employees tell a visitor tend to reflect the way that their company views its character and its culture.

At some companies, the legends in the making involve mad, all-night scrambles to launch a Web site or to release a new piece of software. At other companies, the best lore involves relentless efforts to line up customers. And if a company is attracting favor from venture capitalists or from public shareholders, it's a safe bet that at least one story will involve the shock and delight of employees upon realizing how valuable the business has become.

Employees at CenterBeam Inc., based in Santa Clara, California, could tell variants of all of these stories. Since April 1999, CenterBeam's main service—taking charge of small companies' computer departments by installing networks of wireless, Internet-oriented machines—has attracted hundreds of customers. While CenterBeam hasn't yet gone public, it has attracted ever-higher valuations from VCs and strategic investors. But those aren't the stories that CenterBeam's employees want to tell. Their favorite stories touch on a theme that hardly ever takes center stage in Silicon Valley: integrity—that is, the make-or-break importance of simply keeping your word.

Early on, for example, CenterBeam was on a hiring spree, trying to recruit enough people to carry out its rapid expansion plans. The company offered a job to one candidate, but before that person could accept, a resume from an absolutely dazzling contender arrived. Could the first offer be rescinded, managers wanted to know, so that the company could hire this superstar instead? The answer from Sheldon Laube, 49, CenterBeam's chairman and CEO: No way. "We made a promise to the first candidate," Laube recalls. "If we're going to be the kind of company that people trust, we've got to keep our promises."

Around that same time, CenterBeam executives ordered $500,000 worth of tape drives from a distributor. Those drives (vital equipment that the company uses to back up customer-data files) soon arrived at CenterBeam's headquarters. But before engineers could unpack the merchandise, they learned that a rival distributor was offering comparable machines at a price that would save CenterBeam $93,000 a year. A few engineers wanted to refuse delivery of the more-expensive machines. But CenterBeam executives treated the shipment as binding. Instead, they asked the distributor to take back the expensive system and then bought the cheaper system from the same distributor—at a cost that was roughly $50,000 more than the rival distributor was charging.

What's the road to success for a startup? For many companies, it's whatever road leads them to the most business in the least amount of time. The Internet economy worships at the altar of fast action, fast growth, and fast results. Plenty of companies (and the people who lead them) are prepared to cut a few ethical corners in order to move faster: not gross violations, such as accounting manipulations or outright fraud, but day-to-day dilemmas—leadership moments in which you do either the right thing or the expedient thing. Are you aboveboard with investors when you know that the next quarter may be disappointing? Will you say anything to recruit a great job candidate, or are you honest about the risks involved in an assignment?

If this were a Sunday-school lesson, the answers would be obvious. Virtue would triumph, and cheaters would be vanquished by truth tellers. But the startup business is not so simple. There's a widespread feeling among entrepreneurs and venture capitalists that if a new company doesn't display a bit of bluster and outright exaggeration in its launch phase, it won't be taken seriously—and it won't get a chance to change the world. What fun is starting a company if you can't be a little devious?

Yet if hubris was a winning strategy in the past, its perils have recently become all too clear. Many of the Net companies that went public on the strength of extravagant promises have stumbled badly. In some cases, signs of a credibility gap are so severe that they ooze from companies' financial statements—and translate into plummeting stock prices.

"It's amazing how many employees have come up to me and said, 'It's great to work at a company that has integrity,'" says Laube. "Many employees tell me that at their old companies, 'people promised things that they just didn't deliver.'" Yolanda Gonzalez, 48, VP of human resources at CenterBeam, estimates that two-thirds of the company's new hires tell her that they were uncomfortable with the low ethical standards that prevailed at their former employers.

Some of the clearest thinking about integrity in the Internet economy comes from Darlene Mann, 39, a general partner at Onset Ventures, in Menlo Park, California. Her firm has bankrolled dozens of startups, and she has worked inside numerous high-tech companies. If executives want "integrity" to be more than just a buzzword in a mission statement, she says, they need to think hard about three issues: the growth goals that they promise to customers and investors, the career opportunities that they promise to employees, and the tone that they strike in day-to-day negotiations with business partners. In some cases, Mann acknowledges, keeping one's word carries extra short-term costs. But wiggling away from the truth can be disastrously expensive in the long run.

The point, says Mann, isn't that startups need to let go of their ambitious dreams. But they do need to ensure that promises made to the outside world are believable to their own people. Otherwise, they will be built on a foundation of cynicism and distrust.

What's more, in the current culture of hype, companies that undersell their strengths can win remarkable loyalty. Last year, when Carl Russo was CEO of Cerent Corp., an optical-networking company, he signed up Calico Commerce to build his company's Web site. "Unlike everyone else, they were very subdued in what they promised us," recalls Russo, 44, now a VP and a general manager at Cisco Systems, which recently acquired Cerent. "But they came across as very reliable, trustworthy people." Russo had a good experience with Calico, and now he is one of that company's most valuable customer references.

As the Internet sector undergoes a shakeout of sorts, people are paying a lot of attention to the explicit or implicit promises that companies make to employees and managers. No one ever said that working for an Internet startup was a lifetime job. But some top executives and board members have done a good job of communicating, each step of the way, what could go right and what could go wrong—a practice that makes it easy to regroup when times change. By contrast, other business leaders have opportunistically hired what they thought was a winning growth team, making grand promises without building the kind of stability that gets a company through hard times.

At Onset Ventures, Mann tells some executive recruits to work in their new job for a few months, and to make sure that it will work out, before relocating their families. She also preps candidates on the risks that come with taking a given job. That may make it a little harder to wrap up recruiting efforts in a hurry, but Mann's honesty usually pays off when tough times arise. A person who knows the risks of a job up front, says Mann, "is much more likely to be a good hire in a difficult situation."

Less dramatic, but every bit as challenging, is the issue of how high-tech startups treat their business partners. Perhaps the most common failing of a young, ambitious Internet executive is the tendency to squeeze every possible advantage out of negotiations with an outsider—whether the deal in question involves a $40,000 supply contract or a $20 million marketing alliance. That's just not wise, says Ram Shriram, 43, a former Amazon.com vice president who is now an angel investor. It leaves an undercurrent of bitterness—and a very small list of partners that will want to continue doing business with such a razor-sharp deal maker.

In the long run, argues Scott Sandell, 35, a partner at New Enterprise Associates, a Menlo Park-based venture-capital firm, a more even-handed approach may be the best bet—even in the fast-paced world of Internet negotiations. To illustrate his point, Sandell tells a story of the financing negotiations that got CenterBeam in business. New Enterprise had planned on being one of two firms that would bankroll the business. But at the last moment, a third firm, Accel Partners, swooped in.

That was good news for CenterBeam and for its CEO, Sheldon Laube—but potentially bad news for the earlier investors, who might have ended up getting a smaller stake in the company. Rather than unilaterally reworking CenterBeam's financing terms, Laube asked his early backers if they were willing to add Accel to the financing group. And he didn't revise the deal until they said yes.

According to Sandell, it's all too easy to think that because everything moves so fast in the Internet economy, there just isn't enough time to fuss over the fine points of integrity. In fact, he says, the urgency of Internet-based business means that "there is no time for lack of integrity. Without it, everything becomes more complicated, because you can't depend on people to do what they say they will do."

Sure, we live and work in a world where "the Internet changes everything." But it's heartening to see that some of the Web's smartest mavericks believe that honesty is still the best policy.

George Anders (ganders@fastcompany.com), a *Fast Company* senior editor, is based in Silicon Valley.

DISCUSSION QUESTIONS FOR SECTION 4

1. Which of the companies' stories profiled in this section do you find most compelling?

2. The AES Web site contains valuable information about the firms' values and social role. Do any of the other companies have similarly informative Web sites?

3. Do you think Lego will continue to be a strong international brand? Will they have to alter their rules or values to remain successful?

4. Compare St. Luke's with another advertising agency you know. How are they similar or different?

5. The final selection discusses how "honesty is the best policy" for these firms. What makes their approaches to honesty effective?

ETHICAL BUSINESS LEADERSHIP

This section focuses on the importance of ethics in business leadership. The five articles all examine important, yet quite distinct, aspects of ethical leadership.

The first selection, the "Female CEO" notes differences between female and male top managers. The purpose of including this article here is *not* to propose that all woman managers are superior to men, but rather to emphasize the five points discussed in the article. Each has relevance for ethics. In particular, the fourth, which discusses changing the game, focuses on "honesty." In the wake of Enron and the other recent business scandals, the power of truth and directness of questioning discussed here is of paramount importance to both men and women. Also, this article is included to encourage young women to seek top management posts in the future. One of the drawbacks of the current system is that women are underrepresented at the upper echelons of virtually all corporations. A quotation near the end of the article describes future women managers and their challenges very well:

> Instead, these women seek places to work that value individuals—whether as customers or as employees. They seek places that are transparent and collaborative, that respect relationships at the bedrock of all good businesses. What women want are companies that look a lot more like a network than a pyramid, companies where fairness is a given, companies that value what's ethical above what's expedient.

The second article profiles a specific CEO, Harry Kraemer of Baxter International. The response of Baxter and Kraemer to specific cases that occurred in Madrid and Valencia, Spain and in Croatia, where several patients died after dialysis, is examined. Baxter's core values of respect, responsiveness, and results guided the decision. All employees, not just Kraemer, know what these values mean to the company and why they are practiced religiously at the firm. After a few false starts, Baxter admitted that what happened in Europe was due to a problem at one of the company's plants. Kraemer publicly apologized, and he said, "In the short run, our results are probably worse for the way we handled things. But in the long run, they'll be better. Bad ethics and bad judgment ultimately come back to burn you."

The third article on ethical leadership pertains to the concept of mentoring. Most top executives have had one or more influential mentors who helped them rise in the corporation. Virtue and character ethics has as one of its guiding principles the importance of witnessing and imitating behavior to become a more virtuous person or to have stronger character. Mentoring is a direct application of virtue ethics. This article provides several examples. The "What's in It for Me?" section also examines the three guidelines that a mentor should follow: Believe in the business, make sure you share values, and understand the rewards.

The final two short articles criticize CEO behavior during the past few years. John Ellis (a regular columnist for *Fast Company*) outlines the fall of some CEOs and advocates that business leadership is ultimately a question of ethics. Hammonds interviews CEOs and asks a provocative question: Do CEOs even know right from wrong? Though he is generally critical of recent CEO behavior, the writer challenges CEOs and top managers to know (and not cross) the ethical line.

BY MARGARET HEFFERNAN   FROM *FAST COMPANY* ISSUE 61, PAGE 58

The Female CEO ca. 2002

HERE ARE THE FIVE NAKED TRUTHS ABOUT WOMEN IN BUSINESS. TOGETHER THEY ADD UP TO ONE BIG MESSAGE: THE FUTURE OF BUSINESS DEPENDS ON WOMEN.

Memo
To: All You Businessmen
From: Margaret Heffernan
Re: Can't We Just Work Together?
CC: All Us Businesswomen

Hey, guys! What's the deal with you? You know how important women are—to your businesses as coworkers and as customers and to your lives as, well, fellow human beings—and yet you still can't figure out a reasonable way to work and live with the more than 50% of the world that happens to be us. Well, I think I can help—just by telling you five naked truths about why women still get screwed in the world of business.

But first, I want to tell you a story—and it happens to be a true one.

I was riding on the elevator at work when the doors opened and a young woman got on. After a few seconds of the usual silence, she looked at me and said, "Excuse me. Are you Margaret?"

"Yes," I answered, not knowing what to expect next.

"I just wanted to meet you and shake your hand," she said. "I've never seen a female CEO before."

It's a true story, and it doesn't date from the Middle Ages—or even from last millennium. It happened in Boston in the year 2000 in the offices of CMGI. And what made it remarkable was that it wasn't unusual: Most men and women in business have never seen a female CEO—much less worked with one.

And it looked like we were doing so well! (Or at least that's what we told one another.) More women than ever before hold senior executive positions and sit on corporate boards. Legislation protects pay, maternity leave, and employment rights. The top financial-services firms are busy developing new products and services for a generation of professional women who manage substantial portfolios, who use their tremendous buying power with sharp business acumen, and who will outlive their husbands by a good number of years.

Every one out of four women earns more than her husband. Women control about 80% of household spending and, using their own resources, make up 47% of investors. Women buy 81% of all products and services, buy 75% of all over-the-counter medications, make 81% of retail purchases, and buy 82% of groceries. Women account for 80% of household spending. Eighty percent of the checks written in the

United States are signed by women. Forty percent of all business travelers are women. They are responsible for 51% of all travel and consumer-electronics purchases. Women influence 85% of all automobile purchases. They also head 40% of all U.S. households with incomes over $600,000 and own roughly 66% of all home-based businesses. Women have been the majority of voters in this country since 1964.

Small wonder, then, that car companies and electronics companies are honing their products' designs with women in mind. It makes sense for Fortune magazine to convene an annual conference of powerful women and then to feature Oprah on its cover. Then there's Meg and Carly, Pat and Anne—exhibits A through D to make the case that it's only a matter of time before women reach a state of total equality. And you don't hear women whining anymore, do you?

Well, it all depends on who you talk to. I've spent the past year talking to women, hearing funny, sad, outrageous stories. Those women aren't whining. They're not even complaining. But they do tell a different story than the one that we'd all like to believe.

For example: The wage gap between male and female managers actually widened in the prosperous years between 1995 and 2000. In the communications industry, for instance, a woman earns 73 cents for every $1 a man takes home. Five years earlier, she made 86 cents. The widest pay gap, of course, is between parents. Fathers simply make a lot more than mothers do. Only 4% of the top earners at Fortune 500 companies are women. Women fill only 7.3% of the total line positions held by corporate officers. Where women do hold executive positions, they are more often in management jobs that have relatively lower status—and hence less power. In the past 10 years, the percentage of business-school applicants who are women has not risen at all. It has remained stuck at around 38%. Meanwhile, women are leaving corporate America in droves. And by the way: Between 1992 and 2000, the number of sexual-harassment claims increased by 50%.

What's going on?

During the past 10 years, I have run five businesses, including old-economy and new-economy businesses in both the United States and the United Kingdom. I've hired, fired, and managed hundreds of women (and men) in every discipline and at every level. During the past year, I've interviewed many more women about their careers and their lives—and about the connections or gulfs between the two. What I've learned is just how wrong the conventional wisdom is. Here's the naked truth about women in business today.

1. TOXIC BOSSES STILL CREATE UNFRIENDLY WORK ENVIRONMENTS.

"Neutron Jack" Welch and "Chainsaw Al" Dunlap may have inspired men, but macho leadership styles continue to alienate women. The Boom Boom Room of Smith Barney was more luxurious than the cubicles of software startups, but I've talked to too many women in both environments who have been—and who continue to be—subjected to routine sexual harassment. I've even unwittingly hired some of the perps—liberated guys who definitely know better.

The truth is, the macho exhilaration of coding through the night holds no charm for female engineers. For women executives, racing rental cars around the hotel parking lot is not a cheap thrill. But you will find women enduring these events—sometimes even competing to join them—because they know that it's where the important information always surfaces. When women are asked to name the most significant factors that are holding them back from advancement, the top two answers are "exclusion from informal networks of communication" and "male stereotyping and preconceptions of women."

And it's not just about sex. There's also the money: Men still routinely underpay women and think nothing of it. For years I was the only woman CEO at CMGI. But it wasn't until I read the company's proxy statement that I realized that my salary was 50% of that of my male counterparts. I had the CEO title, but I was being paid as if I were a director.

Of course, I was already accustomed to environments that were riddled with stereotypes. At one point in my career, I received the following email: "I am concerned that you are building a company with too much of a female orientation. We are very strong in female subject promotions and very weak on the male subjects. Your employee population and Board of Directors composition seem to reflect this, as well. For instance, we seem to be strong on promoting gossip, cooking, stars, TV dramas, etc., but much lighter on the major sporting events, business, financial markets, science, autos, etc."

I saved that email. What amazed me about it was that man's preconceptions about "female" and "male" interests. Apparently, women aren't interested in sports, cars, or money.

Here's the bottom line: Toxic bosses claim to like women. But they like them strictly as ornaments, not as power players. Toxic bosses aren't overtly, outrageously sexist—except in occasional emails. And they're not even impossible to work for. But they do poison the atmosphere and pollute the environment. They do create alienating, macho cultures in which it's tough for women to have much fun. Somehow, they can never quite get over their feeling that women in business are charming, submissive, fun to have around, and nice as eye candy—but never quite "one of us."

Which is why women are leaving big companies as fast as they can. By 2005, there will be about 4.7 million self-employed women in the United States, up 77% since 1983. The increase for men? Just 6%. Women leave because they want to work differently and because they don't want to have to add the second job of becoming a change agent to their existing job. Women don't want to redecorate the company. They want to build something new, different, and theirs—from scratch.

2. WOMEN'S CHOICES ARE LIMITED: WHAT'LL IT BE? GEISHA, BITCH, OR GUY?

Everywhere I go, I hear women tell me that in order to progress, women must assimilate. They have to learn to act like a guy. Carly Fiorina's grim stare from the cover of Business Week, complete with cropped hair and dull-gray suit, suggests that assimilation works.

It just doesn't look like much fun. "Of all of the female lawyers who joined my firm when I did, only one remains," one female Boston attorney told me. "And she's just like a guy. I left because I didn't want to play the game."

Not surprisingly, none of the women I've spoken with really wants to be a man. And their stories have made me rethink my own. At one of the companies I ran, a core part of my job was to negotiate agreements with the labor unions. One of the union bosses took me out to lunch at a Chinese restaurant. He used the opportunity to order the most gruesome items on the menu: webbed chicken feet, ducks' tongues, lambs' testicles. The challenge was obvious—and I rose to it. I wasn't about to let him intimidate me; I ate it all. But where I used to tell that story with pride, I now realize that, in a way, I fell into his trap. A far better response to his test would have been to simply order my own dishes, food that I preferred. I should have refused to do the guy thing.

The alternative roles aren't any better. Geishas get jobs because they've got great legs, dress well, or in some way decorate the boss's office. They endure routine flattery—"You're such a treasure!"—and in the process, they end up trivialized. Assertive women get labeled as bitches. There's even a program in California for "bully broads," women whose assertiveness scares men and whose companies send them off to finishing school to learn how to temper their "challenging" behavior. The Taming of the Shrew comes to business.

"You can be a mistress, a daughter, a wife, a mother—or a guy," a high-ranking female property executive told me. Offered such an impoverished range of roles, it's not surprising that women choose the company of other women, creating our own jobs and job descriptions inside organizations that allow us a wider degree of personal expression.

3. YOU CAN'T HAVE IT ALL.

If men and women were truly equal at work, then both genders would hold roughly equal expectations of what is possible—and what isn't. But the truth is, they don't. When it comes to MBAs, fewer women than men get married. And fewer women MBAs have families. On Wall Street, 66% of men with MBAs have families, while 55% of women with MBAs do. The message here is simple: Men and women have very different views of what is manageable—because they have very different management roles.

Women who do have families ultimately find that they have to make other trade-offs, such as giving up private time, friends, hobbies—or ambition. I found that as I gave myself over to my job, I inevitably put my health at risk. It was a choice I had to make: either take time to exercise or give that time to my children.

Women have to give up something, because in dual-income families, women still do most of the child care and the housework. All too often, women collude in their own oppression. They let their mates off easy, holding steadfastly to the sense of power and self-esteem that comes from doing it all—and doing it well. "I like choosing what to cook for everyone," one British woman executive told me. "I like making the lunches and organizing the birthday parties. Does doing it all de-skill my husband? Well, yes. I guess it does."

The most stubbornly optimistic of us still maintain that we can have it all—just not all of it at once. As every woman in the world will tell you, "We all need a wife." But even more than a wife, what every woman I've spoken with yearns for is a life— a whole life, one in which women can be the same people at work that they are at home, with different tasks but with consistent values and styles.

4. WOMEN'S NEW MISSION: CHANGE THE GAME.

Women's goals used to be to get into management, to get onto the boards of Fortune 500 companies, to become CEO. There's a new goal. The aim now is more radical and more ambitious: It is to change the game entirely. Young women pursue a different model, play by different rules. "I love my career, but there are other things in life," one up-and-coming businesswoman told me. "I don't want to be CEO," another said. "I want a whole and healthy life—and even a recession isn't going to scare me into accepting something that isn't me."

When I think back to my career as a CEO, I have to ask: Why did I stay at a place where I was underpaid and subjected to absurd, sexist stereotypes? And when I had a baby, why was I only willing to give myself 10 days of maternity leave? Why would I choose to live like that? The answer I keep coming back to is this: I did those things because I had enough autonomy to create a different kind of culture for all of the people who worked for me. Much more than men, women are painfully aware of the antihuman—and certainly antiwoman—realities that define the contemporary workplace. We feel the harsh conditions, suffer the belittling indignities, battle the sexist innuendos. And we genuinely long for the opportunity to create different structures and different cultures where people can thrive, places where men and women alike can stop faking it and instead unleash their hearts and minds on businesses that respect their capabilities, their commonalities, and their differences.

The truth is, I've heard from plenty of men who talk about having to deal with the idiotic legacy of old-fashioned male stereotypes. Men may not suffer financially and politically the way women do. But the cultural artifacts of a workplace that still operates like a 1950s old-boy network is as frustrating for men as it is for women.

Changing the game starts with honesty. One of my employees at CMGI came to me after a planning meeting at which the refrain was, "Don't tell Margaret." When she had the temerity to ask why I should be kept in the dark, she was told that I was "too honest." The men in the meeting who were advising her were afraid of what might happen if employees really knew what was going on. And they assumed that once I knew, I would share the information with others. What I learned from the story was this: Those men knew, at least intuitively, just how powerful the truth can be. Which is what I told my employee. I said, "There's no more powerful weapon for change than honesty." What she told me in response was, "Now I realize why I love working here. I've always been trusted with the truth, I always knew that I'd get straight answers. This is the first time that I've ever felt really respected at work."

When I talk with women, I'm always struck by their honesty, their directness, and their lack of posturing. Honesty has a way of releasing energy, the kind of energy that business desperately needs to embrace. Time after time, I've witnessed the paralysis that sets in when people are afraid to tell each other the truth. I've come to believe that it's part of the way that men relate to each other in the workplace. For all of their macho posing, most men are simply conflict averse. They don't really want to have an honest disagreement. And so they dodge one another, play turf games, engage in endless rounds of infighting and shadowboxing. They do anything they can to avoid sitting down with one another and telling the truth.

I've encountered CEOs who are unwilling to ask questions, because they're afraid of the answers. I've come into contact with CEOs who are unwilling to tell their direct reports that they are being replaced, because those CEOs are immobilized by the fear of bare emotions, terrified of unscripted conflict. I've seen deals hang in midair, because no one had the honesty to say out loud what everyone was thinking privately: This is really stupid and It will never work. And so millions of dollars and countless hours of work execution, with people in the know hoping that the whole mess will simply go away—but remaining unwilling to address the problem head-on.

Everyone I've spoken with on this matter—male and female alike—knows exactly what I'm talking about when I describe the awkward silence that sets in at corporate meetings when it becomes clear that the emperor has no clothes. Isn't that the most plausible explanation for what went on at Enron? The problem isn't that we don't know the truth. The problem is that we're afraid to speak the truth. Well, the truth is, women are much more likely than men to be truth tellers.

5. WOMEN WORK DIFFERENTLY FROM MEN.

This is the great unspoken truth, the new orthodoxy that every woman I have encountered acknowledges—although usually only in private or with a group of other women. Their caution betrays a fear that is commensurate with the truth: the fear that an acknowledgment of difference will come to mean an acceptance of inequality. A fear that "different from" will morph into "less than."

I don't believe that this is true. I don't believe that we can make meaningful progress as long as we willingly live a lie. More important, the new generation of women won't accept business on its old, dishonest terms.

The Legally Blond generation is not interested in compromise or assimilation. It wears its femininity with pride and seeks success on its own terms. If that success can't be found young women simply won't go there. "If I don't fit into GE or Ford or IBM," one bright young woman told me, "that's not my problem. That's their problem." Rather than fight the system, this next generation of women simply dismisses the system. Instead, these women seek places to work that value individuals—whether as customers or as employees. They seek places that are transparent and collaborative, that respect relationships as the bedrock of all good businesses. What women want are companies that look a lot more like a network than a pyramid, companies where fairness is a given, companies that value what's ethical above what's expedient.

At the same time, this next generation of women is too practical, pragmatic, and tough-minded to be dismissed as ideologues. If they can't find these kinds of companies, then they'll simply build them. What I love about the voices of these women is how they sound: They're not angry, strident, or arrogant—they're profoundly hopeful. These young women may not have seen many female CEOs, but that's just fine. In fact, it's wonderfully liberating. Unintimidated by precedent and unconstrained by convention, these women feel free to create their own style.

Not long ago, I attended yet another conference on business, competition, and where we are in the ongoing evolution of organizations. Needless to say, the speakers were almost all men. But one of them, a senior executive at a major multimedia company, caught my attention. He stood up in public in front of his peers and said, "Our way of doing business is broken."

Oddly enough, I found that admission enormously heartening. That executive said what most of us women already know: that the old command-and-control structures, inspired by or inherited from the military, simply aren't effective. And they are definitely not fun or inspiring. As I watch my female colleagues leave traditional business structures, as I see them flourish, as I notice how well networks protect women through a recession and how brutally men suffer from the harsh cutbacks and relentless downsizings that rumble through corporate hierarchies, it strikes me that women are building a parallel business universe. It's one in which companies work differently, one in which lives are lived honestly—a world of work where lives are integrated, not delegated.

If our way of doing business is indeed broken—and if the collapse of Enron, Andersen, Global Crossing, Kmart, and others are just the symptoms—then we had all better hope that this parallel universe is almost complete. We may need it sooner than we thought we would. And it sure looks like a lot more fun.

Margaret Heffernan (margaret_heffernan@hotmail.com) is writing a book on the naked truths about women in business.

BY KEITH H. HAMMONDS   FROM *FAST COMPANY* ISSUE 64, PAGE 93

Harry Kraemer's Moment of Truth

IN AN ERA WHEN THE BUSINESS SECTION READ LIKE THE POLICE BLOTTER, THE CEO OF BAXTER INTERNATIONAL FACED A TOUGH ETHICAL DILEMMA. AND HE DID SOMETHING NOTEWORTHY: HE ACTUALLY DID THE RIGHT THING.

As far as anyone knows, the first few deaths occurred in Madrid starting on August 15, 2001.

The Spanish patients, two men and two women, were elderly and very ill. All four had undergone routine dialysis at the Hospital de la Princesa. Soon after, they began sweating and vomiting, some of them in excruciating pain. They died within a few hours of receiving treatment.

Nothing seemed exceptional about the deaths of those old, sick patients on dialysis, even though four deaths had occurred in four days at the same place. Hospital officials notified the manufacturers of the equipment involved, as dictated by protocol. But no one paid the incident much attention—until the following week, when people started dying in Valencia.

As in Madrid, the six patients who died after dialysis at the clinic Virgen del Consuelo were mostly old and sick. But they had one more thing in common. It was inconclusive evidence, but regional health officials told the media anyway: The dialysis Filters used in all of the cases had come from a single lot—the same lot as the Filters used in Madrid. They had been manufactured by Althin Medical AB, which had been acquired in March 2000 by the American company Baxter International Inc.

The U.S. business press didn't report much on the situation. News of the deaths was soon eclipsed, first by the profound tragedy of September 11 and then by the opening bars of Enron's opera of greed and deceit. Over the next few weeks, though, a total of 53 deaths in the United States and six other countries would be linked circumstantially to Baxter's filters. It wasn't clear until later that the filters were to blame. To this day, it isn't clear exactly what went wrong.

But what was certain was this: Baxter and its CEO, Harry M. Jansen Kraemer Jr., faced a moment of truth. How Baxter responded would leave a lasting imprint on the company's relationships with patients and doctors, with employees, and, of course, with investors. The episode would, for better or worse, open a window onto Baxter's corporate soul.

What did Harry Kraemer do? He did something that feels unusual—subversive, almost—in light of the air of mistrust and criminality that pervades big business.

"When in the past nine months have you ever heard a corporate executive apologize?" marvels William W. George, the recently retired CEO of medical-instrument maker Medtronic Inc. The answer: almost never.

Baxter's response to its filter crisis wasn't perfect. But Baxter's CEO owned up to the situation. He told the truth. He took responsibility when it would have been easy not to. His company took a $189 million hit, and he recommended that the board reduce his bonus. In other words, Kraemer did the right thing.

"THERE WAS TOO MUCH THERE TO BE A COINCIDENCE"

Baxter International is a $7.7 billion company with 48,000 employees. Founded in 1931 by Dr. Don Baxter to manufacture and distribute intravenous solutions, it still sells IV bags as well as biopharmaceuticals and drug-delivery systems. Its products treat millions of patients a year who suffer from hemophilia, infectious diseases, and cancer.

The thing about selling all of those drugs, devices, and solutions is that a lot can go wrong. Nearly every product that Baxter delivers is a matter of life and death. But when the outcome is death, it can be incredibly difficult to determine a treatment's effectiveness. Was the death normal and predictable? Or did the treatment somehow fail? The answers aren't always obvious. If medical-products companies pulled their wares every time someone died, there would be no medical products.

That is the reason why, even as Baxter quickly recalled the lot of filters associated with the patient deaths in Spain, it did not at first accept responsibility. The recall was a sensible precaution, no more. And on October 9, Baxter announced the results of a set of internal analyses, plus another set commissioned of an independent consultant. There was, in fact, no evidence that the dialysis filters in Spain had malfunctioned in any way. Nor had the clinics' water supplies been contaminated. Basically, the deaths remained unexplained.

But that Saturday morning, October 13, Alan Heller checked his voice mail from his hotel in San Francisco, where he was attending a conference. Heller had joined Baxter less than a year before to serve as president of its $1.9 billion renal division. The Althin operation, acquired to complement Baxter's existing dialysis products, was part of his business.

The phone message was shocking. Newspapers and television in Croatia were reporting that 23 dialysis patients had died during the previous week at clinics across the country. The government was blaming Baxter.

The studies that were done after the deaths in Spain had exonerated the dialyzers. But The filters in Croatia were probably manufactured around the same time as the ones in Spain. What's more, the recent deaths had occurred at six locations, and the patients weren't all elderly. The clustering in two different countries was highly unusual. Something was wrong with the filters.

Suddenly, Baxter's world exploded. The deaths were front-page news every day in the Croatian newspapers. The Croatian health ministry, like regional officials in Valencia, refused to release the used filters to Baxter for testing. The possibility of tampering was broached.

For Heller, the first decision was obvious. He ordered a global recall of all of Althin's filters and a distribution hold on the ones that had already been made. The action, Heller says, cost Baxter about $10 million. "But the cost was minimal compared to the potential cost to patients if we went ahead with the product," Heller says. Clearly, too, Baxter's legal liability would have been enormous if it had failed to act and more patients died.

Heller assigned Marla Persky to head an internal task force charged with confronting the debacle. Persky, a deputy general counsel who was responsible for the renal division's legal and government affairs, had overseen the integration of the Althin acquisition. Persky pulled in staffers worldwide from quality, manufacturing, toxicology, marketing, communications, clinical affairs, and other departments. That evening, the team of 27 gathered for their first conference call. They would talk twice a day for the next month, working to identify the gaps in their information and where they needed expertise. They hired forensic toxicologists to reexamine the returned filters. They combed through documents, hoping to find anything—a change in the manufacturing process, a new supplier, perhaps different packaging.

And they found nothing. Neither did a team of European physicians assembled by Baxter. Finally, a quality engineer in Althin's Ronneby, Sweden plant noticed something unusual about one of the recalled filters. At one end of the device, between the fibers and a potting compound, were a few bubbles. The bubbles weren't supposed to be there.

A dialysis filter is a disposable product that costs less than $15. The technology is pretty straightforward. At Althin, each filter was tested several times before shipping. An air test determined whether there were any leaks. For the 10% of filters that did leak, workers injected a solution to locate the problem for repair. That solution was supposed to be vacuumed and evaporated from the filters. But the bubbles were evidence that trace amounts of the liquid remained. The solution, made by 3M, had been labeled as nontoxic—and chemically, it was. But when heated to body temperature in a patient's bloodstream, the toxicologists theorized, it gasified, causing a fatal pulmonary embolism.

No one at Baxter knew why the solution was removed from some filters and not others. The apparent randomness made little sense. "Why now?" Persky remembers wondering. "Why not a year earlier? Why not for other manufacturers?" Why wasn't the solution tested for reaction to temperature? Because 3M never intended it to come into contact with anyone's bloodstream. Why was it used at Ronneby? Because the contractor who designed the process there had done the same thing for another company. Why hadn't the earlier analyses identified the problem? Because when technicians opened the filters for testing, the trace liquid evaporated.

"There will always be a thousand 'why's," Persky says now. "So we had to focus on the 'what.'" And on November 2, when test results confirmed Baxter's working hypothesis, the what became unavoidable. Rabbits injected with the 3M solution had nearly died, exhibiting the same symptoms as the patients in Spain and Croatia. The following morning, a Saturday, Heller called Kraemer at home to lay out the situation. Kraemer was packing the car for a camping trip with his daughter. Heller reported on the animal tests and their implications. He explained Baxter's options. After a discussion about Baxter's likely strategy, Kraemer told Heller, "Let's make sure we do the right thing." Then he went camping.

"WHAT HARRY SAYS HE BELIEVES IN"

What is it, exactly, that makes Kraemer so different from your typical big-company CEO? He has a rumpled, boyish look to him, resembling the actor Michael Keaton in dowdy pinstripes and a button-down shirt. He is an accountant by training, with an MBA from Northwestern's Kellogg School of Management. He is a Midwestern native and a devout Catholic. He drives a Toyota Avalon.

It's not any of that. What separates Kraemer from most CEOs you've read about is this: He is relentlessly authentic. He tells the truth, and he acts on his beliefs. "There are relatively few people in the world like Harry," says Donald P. Jacobs, dean emeritus at the Kellogg School. "Harry lives his life the way most of us would like to live our lives. What Harry says he believes in, you can put it in the bank. The way he treats his coworkers is the way he'd like people to treat him."

Kraemer has attracted attention for his vocal insistence that he remain a deeply involved dad to his five children—and for his hope that others at Baxter will get a life too. But that's just part of the deal. What he's done in a short time at Baxter is change the way an entire company thinks.

Back in 1993, Baxter International pled guilty to cooperating illegally with an Arab boycott of Israel. That same year, the U.S. Department of Veterans Affairs temporarily banned Baxter from selling to its hospitals, alleging that the company fraudulently oversold products to the government. Around that time, Baxter put forth a set of "shared values" for the company: respect, responsiveness, and results. The response would have seemed like typical corporate window dressing, a predictable, shallow response to public scrutiny, but for the guy who directed the effort: Baxter's newly appointed, 38-year-old chief financial officer, Harry Kraemer.

Respect, responsiveness, results—people at Baxter actually believe that stuff. "Do the right thing"—Kraemer repeats it ad nauseum. So does everyone else. People know what it means. And it sticks. That's why Kraemer could drive off that Saturday confident that Heller would act responsibly. "If I didn't think Al would do the right thing on this one, I had a much bigger issue," he says.

Do the right thing. "We have this situation," Kraemer continues, describing the filter crisis. "The financial people will assess the potential financial impact. The legal people will do the same. But at the end of the day, if we think it's a problem that a Baxter product was involved in the deaths of 50 people, then those other issues become pretty easy. If we don't do the right thing, then we won't be around to address those other issues.

"I'm not a very smart guy, so let's keep it simple. Think of any problem you need to deal with. There are a million pieces of information that can get involved in a decision. But let's get above the tree line and ask some simple questions. What is the issue? What are the alternatives? What are the pros and cons? What is the best solution? Life is complex, but you can boil the morass down to thinking simply."

"THIS PROBLEM WILL NEVER HAPPEN AGAIN"

Baxter could have ducked the blame. It could have pulled the filters ever so quietly from the market—and since the line accounted for less than $20 million in revenue, it's likely that few would have noticed. With some justification, it could have blamed Althin's former owner, since Baxter had only recently taken over the business. It could have blamed 3M, for that matter. It could have faulted the lack of cooperation from Croatian and Valencian authorities.

Too often, that is how it works in business. "You bring in lawyers and PR companies, and you find ways to say, 'This is not our fault,'" says Brad Googins, executive director of the Center for Corporate Citizenship at Boston College. Companies and their executives duck, shirk, and deny. And in doing so, they destroy trust.

On November 5, 2001, Baxter announced that it had identified the probable cause of the dialysis-patient deaths. In a press release, Kraemer made this statement: "We are greatly saddened by the patient deaths and I would like to extend my personal sympathies to family members of those patients. We have a responsibility to make public our findings immediately and take swift action, even though confirmatory studies remain under way."

Baxter could have stopped selling only the 10% of filters that needed repair. After all, those were the only ones in which the solution had been used. But the tragedy had compromised the entire Althin brand. And Baxter didn't have all of the facts; it never did see the filters from Croatia. Perhaps some patients had died from filters that hadn't been exposed to the solution. "Were we 100% confident?" Kraemer asks. "No. We didn't know."

So Baxter shut down Althin for good. It closed the factory in Ronneby and another in Florida. It took a charge to earnings of $189 million to cover the costs of the closure and its anticipated settlements with the families of patients who had died. By year's end, it would pay the Spanish families a reported $290,000 each. (The company won't confirm the amount or disclose the sums paid to families in Croatia, who also have settled.) The lone suit involving an American patient has also been resolved. The plaintiff's attorney in the case, Kenneth Moll, says that Baxter "behaved appropriately and responsibly."

The next day, Kraemer and Heller flew to Washington, DC to brief officials at the Food and Drug Administration on the company's findings and its plan of action. Baxter executives had similar conversations with regulators in Spain, Croatia, and other affected countries. Baxter had warned 3M of the problem over the weekend. It also had reported the problem with the dialysis filters to rival manufacturers it knew or suspected were using the same process.

In the months that followed, Baxter searched through records for hundreds of thousands of its products and product parts, looking for processes that might resemble the faulty one at Ronneby. It added steps to qualify any material used in manufacturing, even if that material wasn't designed to stay in the end product. "This made us second-guess systems that we'd had for 20 years and that had always worked," Persky says. Adds Jose Divino, the associate medical director who had been

Baxter's point man in Spain and Croatia: "What we know for sure is, this problem will never happen again."

And there was one more thing. Kraemer recommended that the compensation committee of Baxter's board of directors reduce his performance bonus by at least 40% for 2001. (In the end, he still got paid $1.4 million.) He also suggested to the committee that his top executives take a 20% cut. Patients had died on their watch. They had been responsible.

So Baxter admitted that it was wrong. It took the hit. And guess what? The world didn't end. The company's stock dropped slightly on news of the charge to earnings but soon recovered. "Baxter didn't try to assign blame away," says David Lothson, an analyst who follows Baxter for UBS Warburg LLC. "It showed signs of dealing with it decisively rather than letting it drag on. Investors tend to react very favorably to that."

The message to CEOs: Investors like honesty, including public apologies. (Kraemer visited New York to apologize in person to the president of Croatia.) So, it turns out, do employees. Kraemer was flooded with appreciative emails and phone messages from Baxter workers. As for customers, Heller admits that his renal business has dropped off in Europe—but he hopes to win that back too. "We violated the physicians' trust," he says. "It wasn't intentional, but our product failed. We have to rebuild that trust."

"In the short run," Heller allows, "our results are probably worse for the way we handled things. But in the long run, they'll be better. Bad ethics and bad judgment ultimately come back to burn you." (Of course, good ethics don't guarantee safe passage either. At press time, the FDA announced that on September 6, 2002, Baxter notified hemodialysis centers that tubing and needles used with its dialysis machines might have been linked to five deaths in the United States in late August.)

Nearly a year after the first death in Spain, Kraemer sits in his office, pondering the aftermath. To him, there is nothing extraordinary about what Baxter has done. This is simply how organizations and their people should behave. "Simplicity," he says. "Open communication of values." Respect, responsiveness, results. "Over and over and over again." If the values are authentic, then so are the decisions and the actions.

He pauses, then finishes the thought. "Of course we'll do the right thing," he says. "As opposed to what?"

Keith H. Hammonds (khammonds@fastcompany.com) is a *Fast Company* senior editor based in New York. Learn more about Baxter International on the Web (http://www.baxter.com).

WHAT'S FAST

Confidence and Humility

Handcuffs have replaced cuff links as the most visible wrist wear for CEOs—which makes Baxter International CEO Harry Kraemer's philosophy of leadership all the more refreshing.

"Leadership is a delicate blend of self-confidence and humility. You have to have the self-confidence to say, 'You don't want to make that decision without my input!'

"But self-confidence without humility becomes a problem. I may be the CEO. But part of that was having a few skills, and part of it was luck. Part of it was the man upstairs. So I'm no better than anyone else. Self-confidence and humility: Blend those two together, and you have someone who has a good chance of leading effectively.

"Ninety-nine percent of people want to do the right thing. I've got 48,000 employees, most of whom care about the environment, or they have parents, or they are parents. I'm representing them. I've got 48,000 people who assume that we're going to do the right thing."

BY JENNIFER REINGOLD   FROM *FAST COMPANY* ISSUE 42, PAGE 58

Want to Grow as a Leader? Get a Mentor!

EVEN TOP EXECUTIVES NEED MENTORS—AND SOMETIMES THE BEST MENTORS WORK ELSEWHERE.

When it comes to understanding the fine points of a balance sheet, Mack Tilling is no rookie. The cofounder and CEO of Instill Corp., a business-to-business technology company for the food-service industry, founded the Redwood City-based outfit in 1993—long before b2b became the flavor of the month.

So why does Tilling, 36, get so fired up when he talks about his monthly breakfasts with his mentor, David Garrison, CEO of Verestar Communications and former head of Netcom? Because, Tilling says, being able to talk about your work with an experienced executive can help anyone—even a CEO—make better decisions. "Mentors help you see things in a way that you might not have thought about," he says. "They've all been there many times before, often under diverse and challenging circumstances."

It's no news flash, of course, that there is value in the relationship between a mentor and a "mentee." But finding a mentor is usually an informal affair. And often, mentorships develop between junior- and senior-level employees at the same company. At Instill, however, this isn't just an ad hoc process; it's part of an innovative plan for leadership development. All senior executives are asked to choose a mentor whom they admire, usually an executive at another company who is in the same functional area. Mentors must be approved by the Instill board, must sign confidentiality and no-conflict agreements, and are asked to meet with their mentees at least once a quarter. In exchange for their commitment, they are offered a small amount of stock in Instill.

By all reports, the program has been a rousing success. So far, five of Instill's nine executives have mentors, and all say that the relationships have had a huge impact on their effectiveness as managers. That is due in no small part to the fact that their mentors are high-level people with impressive track records: Rocky Pimentel, for example, senior vice president of WebTV Networks Inc., mentors Eric Ludwig, Instill's VP of finance and administration; Andy Cohen, Instill's VP of marketing, has teamed up with Mohanbir Sawhney, professor of e-commerce and technology at Northwestern University's Kellogg Graduate School of Management and a member of five corporate boards; and Dan Dorosin, Instill's VP of corporate development, is mentored by Paul Lego, president and CEO of Virage Inc.

Clearly, Instill is onto something: In the roughly 30 months since the program was started, no mentor approached by an Instill executive has refused the opportunity to participate. The stock offer is arguably a significant factor in that success rate. But since Instill has no immediate plans to go public, it seems equally clear that the promise of a huge financial reward is not what is persuading mentors to sign on.

In fact, Virage's Lego, 42, says that he would have agreed to mentor Dorosin even without the stock offer. "I enjoy mentoring," he says. "Why do people teach? It's not for the money." Structure also makes a difference to Lego: "The program makes me more conscious of the relationship and of keeping up my end of the obligation."

Despite going after folks with multiple board positions and demanding day jobs, all Instill executives have gotten their first choice. But that hasn't happened by accident. The Instill search process—equal parts matchmaking and due diligence—works because the would-be mentees are approaching people with whom they can cultivate a personal and professional chemistry.

"I have developed an affinity for Eric," says WebTV's Pimentel, 45, of Ludwig. "The driving factor is my sense of responsibility to him."

Similarly, Verestar's Garrison says that it was his fundamental respect for Tilling's company—coupled with his own sense of been there, done that, could have used that—that made him decide to say yes when Tilling popped the question. "As a CEO, in many ways, you live in a bubble," says Garrison, 45. "It's difficult to find someone in whom you can have complete confidence and confidentiality."

And the rewards for the Instill executives are palpable. In addition to helping Andy Cohen, 37, develop a more strategic marketing plan, Mohanbir Sawhney has used his clout to introduce his mentee to such food-industry big shots as Jack Greenberg, chairman and CEO of McDonald's. "The board is usually beating up on you, not coaching you," says Cohen. "This is a nice bonus that I've never had at another company."

Contact Mack Tilling by email (info@instill.com).

WHAT'S IN IT FOR ME?

Is being a mentor simply a labor of love, or can you get something back in the process? Verestar Communications CEO David Garrison discusses his relationship with Mack Tilling, CEO of Instill Corp.—and how to make being a mentor work for you.

Believe in the Business

One of the reasons that Garrison agreed to become Tilling's mentor was because he appreciated Instill's business model. "You have to believe in the business. Otherwise, you're helping to train an athlete in a race that goes nowhere."

Make Sure You Share Values

Garrison has been surprised and pleased to become friends with Tilling. "We have connected on a personal level, and he is a delight. He's a great human being, very smart and fun to be with." Although Garrison doesn't think that mentors need to be best friends with their mentees, he does think that both partners should feel simpatico on some level. So if there's not a basic understanding, don't try to be a mentor. You won't do a good job.

Understand the Rewards

As a CEO and a board member at two other companies, Garrison is a busy guy. But he says that being a mentor to Tilling has been deeply rewarding. "If you can help people develop a skill set, then you can take immense personal satisfaction when they do a good job. In a board setting, you are one of 7 to 10 people, as opposed to being in a one-on-one situation." In a mentoring situation, he says, the question is, "How can I help this person train himself to be even more of a winner?"

Contact David Garrison by email (david_garrison@verestar.com).

A Monthly Column on Strategy

Just two years ago, he was the master of all he surveyed. He chaired the board meetings. He was paid in the millions. He graced the covers of magazines. He was smart, he had vision, he was tough as nails. He was a leader of the global business revolution. He was the CEO.

Now he sits alone in his office. His assistant holds all of his calls. CNBC is on television, and the news is not good. The press has turned ugly. The ingrates on the board have asked him to move up the next scheduled meeting. Regulators see him as a potential target. Politicians look at him as an issue. Investors assume that everything he says is self-serving nonsense. And the poor bastard is paralyzed. He can't believe it. He asks himself, "How can this be happening?"

The question is the answer. It's happening because it turns out that these Masters of the Universe, these magazine cover boys, have revealed themselves to be ... simpering yuppie wimps. If adversity is the test of character, then so far, today's CEOs are failing miserably. By turns disagreeable, petulant, and self-pitying, they have as a group failed their employees, their investors, and their customers. They border on the pathetic.

Here's what real business leaders do. They go out and rally the troops, plant the flag, and make a stand. They confront hostile audiences, and they deal with the press. They go after the short sellers. If the issue is confidence, they conduct themselves confidently. If the issue is trust, they make their company's business transparent. If the issue is character, they tell the truth. They do not shirk responsibility; they assume command.

Here's what leaders *don't* do. They don't blame underlings. They don't blame their predecessor. They don't complain about press coverage. They don't whine about Wall Street. They don't mindlessly cut research and development. They don't fire 4,000 people in the hope that it will bump up their company's stock for the weekend. They don't obfuscate, dissemble, or lie. They don't hide behind a retinue of handlers and lawyers and public-relations fools.

In the realm of publicly owned companies, nothing so perfectly captures the fiber of today's whimpering CEOs than the stock-buyback announcement. Stock buybacks are step one in rebuilding confidence in a publicly traded company. After a dive in the company's stock price, the CEO announces that, while everyone else is selling that stock, his company is planning to repurchase as much of the stock as it can afford. *He* knows the value of the enterprise. *He* knows all the numbers. And *he* is willing to bet on it. Stock buybacks are insider trading at its best-they send a clear signal that management believes that the company's prospects are bright.

Except that today's CEOs aren't following through. They're saying that they'll do it, but the likelihood is that they probably won't. And everybody knows it! The people who run mutual funds and those who work at high-powered investment firms think that fewer than half of the announced company-buyback plans will actually occur. While many have been announced, probably 6 out of 10 are nothing more than public-relations gimmicks.

How about that? In the middle of an epidemic of corporate scandal, dishonesty, and malfeasance, the first response of a large number of current CEOs is to *lie*. What are these people thinking? It's *public* information. And it will make a great little story, the perfect box score: Here's what they said they were going to do, and here's what they actually did. (As it happens, the *Wall Street Journal* is keeping score.)

Another behavioral pattern of the new breed of wimp CEOs is the disappearing act. How many CEOs of major Wall Street investment firms have directly addressed the (politely phrased) issue of "investor confidence"? That would be one. Henry Paulson of Goldman Sachs spoke at the National Press Club in Washington and actually took questions after his speech. None of the others have said a word, except in carefully worded advertisements in the *Wall Street Journal* and the *New York Times*. They haven't been struck dumb. They're hiding.

When CEOs hide out together, another behavioral pattern of the new breed emerges. You might call it the "Wall Street whine." It goes something like this. Not so long ago, Wall Street demanded managed earnings (steady, predictable growth). No managed earnings, no rising stock price. Now Wall Street says that it doesn't want managed earnings, it wants the numbers unpolished. So CEOs deliver unpolished earnings, and Wall Street hammers the stock on slow or no quarterly growth. The wimpy CEO chorus bellows, "Not fair!" Poor lambs. The evil meanies went and changed the rules on you.

Lying, hiding, whining—what are we missing here? Oh yes, blame assessment. Over lunch, I recently gave a talk to executives from one of the world's great financial supermarkets about the upcoming midterm elections. After I finished my remarks, they gave me their views on what had gone wrong. It came down to one name: Paul O'Neill (the secretary of the treasury). It was all his fault. If Robert Rubin was still in there, none of this would have happened. I think they actually believed what they were saying.

The good news is that not all CEOs are behaving this way. General Electric's Jeff Immelt, Berkshire Hathaway's Warren Buffett, and Microsoft's Bill Gates aren't lying, hiding, whining, or blame-shifting. They're fighting the good fight. They're alive to the opportunities of the current economic turmoil. Their companies will emerge from all of this as winners. Because a fundamental ingredient of business success is leadership. And the granular stuff of leadership is courage, conviction, and character.

John Ellis (jellis@fastcompany.com), a writer and consultant, works in media, politics, and technology. Read his weekday musings on the Web (www.johnellis.blogspot.com).

BY KEITH H. HAMMONDS   FROM *FAST COMPANY* ISSUE 63, PAGE 81

The Secret Life of the CEO: Do They Even Know Right from Wrong?

WHY SO MANY GOOD EXECUTIVES MAKE SO MANY TERRIBLE CHOICES. THE HIGH STAKES, THE PRESSURE TO PERFORM, AND THE TEMPTATION TO GO FOR THE DOUGH ARE PART OF THE PROBLEM.

Perhaps we understand now. Or we're starting to. The corporate CEO is not the epic hero we once imagined. Now we know: He was never as smart or as right or as, well, together as we had hoped. His teeth aren't perfect either. But let's not go overboard: He's also not an epic sociopath. CEOs are only as culpable for all that has gone wrong with business in the past year as they were responsible for all that went right in the previous years. Which is to say that whatever they have done or failed to do doesn't explain everything. It doesn't even explain most things.

The truth behind the current episode of corporate comi-tragedy has plenty to do with the men (and they are mostly men) who are running the show—but not in the way that we've always thought. All of our post-Enron hand-wringing about CEOs having values and "walking the talk" isn't wrong, exactly. It's just that it's not exactly right either. The truth is more shaded than that.

The truth is this: CEOs are flawed individuals who are operating in a complex, imperfect world. They are no more or less honest than the rest of us—in fact, "honesty" almost misses the point. The point is, they negotiate a razor's edge between knowing one thing and having to say another.

They are intensely driven to achieve and they operate in a marketplace that measures achievement almost wholly in the short term. They confront a world that moves faster than ever before, and really, there is little about their unwieldy organizations that they easily control.

It's not that we've suddenly promoted a new generation of CEOs who are somehow badly flawed. On paper, these CEOs are pretty much the same as the ones who ran companies a decade ago. Today's average big-company CEO is 56 years old, is male, and has been with his company for 18 years, according to a survey by Chief Executive magazine and head-hunting firm Spencer Stuart Inc. As a group, they are very well educated: Thirty-seven percent have MBAs. They know numbers, and they understand the inner workings of their companies: Some 22% have come up through finance, and another 14% have toiled in operations. That's not what's different.

What's different is the sandbox that today's CEOs play in. The sand started shifting in 1993, the year that professional managers took on investors—and lost. In the same week, the CEOs of American Express, IBM, and Westinghouse all resigned under pressure—basically because their companies' financial results were lousy. In the years that followed, executive pay was increasingly tied to company performance: More stock; more options.

For a while, that sort of accountability seemed like a pretty good thing. But in the late 1990s, stocks soared—and so did investors' expectations. If you were a CEO, and you cared about your stock price and your own paycheck, you heeded the complaints and demands of the research analyst s at big brokerages whose utterances could send your stock into orbit—or down the drain. Says William George, who retired in May as chairman of Medtronics Inc.: "The pressure is always with you. You can't escape it, even for an hour."

"It was unrealistic," says David Nadler, chairman of Mercer Delta Consulting and adviser to a number of big-time CEOs. "But if you were the CEO, there was the perception that if you slipped, your stock price could plunge. There was the temptation to think, 'If this is a short-term problem, I can shore it up.' There are tremendous temptations from the system to cut corners."

In the face of such demand for short-term results, you could shore up your business. Or you could try. But in real life, big-company CEOs only wield so much authority. "We're just human beings running battleships, and battleships don't turn easily," says Stephen Berger, a former top executive at GE Capital who now heads Odyssey Investment Partners LLC.

For all that's written about CEO charisma, power, and authority, chief executives, it turns out, rarely can make their companies change through an executive edict. Instead, they build coalitions and seek consensus. "A CEO doesn't make decisions," says the founder of one of the most prominent dotcoms of the 1990s. "The job is mostly the art of balancing interests and dealing with shades of gray. CEOs are often frustrated because they can see where they want to take the organization, but they can't get the organization to go there."

Here, then, is the true essence of the CEO syndrome: It's not that chief executives are especially dishonest, corrupt, or inept. The real problem is, they're alone.

"Being a CEO really is a lonely job," says James Maxmin, who has headed Laura Ashley PLC, the consumer-electronics branch of Thorn EMI, and Volvo UK. "With your subordinates and your peers, you need to have a degree of detachment. There's some detachment from your board too, because they are evaluating you. So you become cocooned in your own self-importance."

So let's get down to it: *Are CEOs honest?* Well, define honest. Do most CEOs lie through their teeth? Enron's Jeffrey Skilling sure pushed the envelope. But for most CEOs, the answer is no. On the other hand, are most CEOs steeped in institutional corporate-speak? Do they find a way to walk the line between saying just enough, not too much, and never the wrong thing? You bet.

After all, how do you tell employees that business is likely worse than it seems? That layoffs are imminent? When do you let customers know that you're going to make their installed products obsolete? Often, you just don't.

"There's a lot you can't share with anyone," says Anne Mulcahy, the well-regarded president and CEO of Xerox Corp. "I've tried to be fair and honest in my approach, letting people know what to expect. But there's information that you have to retain while keeping up the image that you're feeling no anxiety inside." And while CEOs today are under the microscope when it comes to telling the truth, how much truth is too much? Mulcahy found out on October 3, 2000, when she proclaimed Xerox's business model to be "unsustainable." Mulcahy was trying to be forthright. But her company's stock dropped 26% that day. "That was a painful lesson," Mulcahy says now.

And so, the razor's edge. You are a CEO. You have the title, the visibility, and the responsibility. You're also isolated. You're under extraordinary pressure to deliver results. And you're deathly afraid of failing.

So do CEOs fudge the numbers?

Of course they do. Add it up: There's the pressure, the scrutiny, and the generally accepted accounting practices (which institutionalize a set of standards that don't so much define what must be done as establish the boundaries of how far you can go). Suddenly, playing with the numbers doesn't seem so bad. "It's increasingly difficult to stand up and say, 'I made a mistake,'" says Maxmin, whose new book, *The Support Economy: Why Corporations Are Failing Individuals and the Next Episode of Capitalism* (Viking Penguin, 2002), derives in part from his own conflicted corporate experience. "One way to show that I never make mistakes is to deliver consistently higher earnings. And one way to do that is with reserve accounting. I knew plenty of executives who thought that it was perfectly proper to have next year's profit—or most of it—already reserved. You're on a treadmill, and you become more and more creative."

"Do you sometimes try to manage the numbers?" asks Berger. "Yeah." After all, part of what investors expect from CEOs is a best-case financial argument on behalf of the company. But at what point do the best-case scenarios become false accounting practices?

"There's a moment," Berger says. "You're sitting with the independent auditors, and everyone leaves the room—except for the audit committee. And you say, 'Give me the skinny.' And the auditors say, 'There are two or three things that we're negotiating with management.' There's nothing wrong with that. But you have to ask the next question: What are those things? And then you have to go back to the managers and tell them, 'You're right' or 'You're wrong.' The decision itself is gray—but the decision process should be very clear."

And so here's the real question: *Do CEOs even know right from wrong?*

You have just had to manipulate your financials to make your numbers—anything to keep the analysts smiling. And after you've fudged the financials, you find ways to justify the crime—did I say "crime"?—I meant the *practice*. It's really not hard. "There are things that happen when you join a company that cause you to believe that the values in one's outside life aren't relevant any more on the inside," says Jeffrey Pfeffer, a professor of organizational behavior at Stanford's Graduate School of Business. "You say, 'The rules are different, and life is complex.' So what has been going on recently really has more to do with an unsurpassed ability on the part of senior corporate leaders to justify anything."

It's no surprise that no one—not Mulcahy, not Maxmin—admits to bending (much less breaking) the rules in illegal or unethical ways. "It's not that complex," says Berger. "If you don't know where the line is by the time you're a CEO, you shouldn't be in that office." Larry Bossidy, the driven and hard-driving former CEO of Honeywell, swears that he never made an ethical decision that left him feeling uncomfortable. "You can't do that," he says flatly.

Maybe. Or maybe CEOs simply feel comfortable with more nuance than the rest of us do. Perhaps being a CEO means that you have an uncanny ability to operate in an ethical murkiness that would drown most people. Perhaps the secret of living with yourself as a big-company CEO lies in seeing all of the grays as blacks and whites. Perhaps the good news about all of today's CEO scandals is that, finally, we're getting closer to the truth about the secret lives of CEOs.

Keith H. Hammonds (khammonds@fastcompany.com) is a *Fast Company* senior editor based in New York.

THE COMIC: DEFENSE ATTORNEY FOR THE DAMNED

Meet Emily Levine

Emily Levine is equal parts philosopher and comic. In her celebrated career, Levine has been part of an improv comedy group, written for television sitcoms, done stand-up comedy, and wrote and performed an Emmy-winning series of commercial satire segments for television. She has earned the greatest praise for her one-woman shows, *"Myself, Myself, I'll Do It Myself,"* and, last month, *"Common cen$e."* According to the executive producers of The Sopranos, "If Einstein came back as a stand-up comic, he'd be Emily Levine."

Ladies and gentlemen of the jury: I rise before you in defense of the damned.

Let's consider this case on its merits. The prosecution has argued that my clients misstated earnings, overvalued their worth, overreached, overweened, and carried out the wholesale hijacking of their companies' assets—motivated solely by greed. This we categorically deny. Greed was not the sole motivation. Yes, these CEOs wanted more money, bigger cars, multiple mansions, fatter bank accounts, limitless perks, and free stock options—for starters. But they sought those baubles for a reason that was far more elemental than greed. The basis for my clients' actions was, in fact, nothing less than the laws of physics. My clients, big men all, were merely keeping faith with the dictates of an even larger force: the universe.

According to cosmologists, the universe began as a tiny dot that exploded suddenly and that has been expanding—and will continue to expand—for billions and billions of years. I ask the 12 of you seated in the jury box to put yourselves in the shoes of a CEO—say, Jack Welch. You come face-to-face with this vision of limitless expansion for the first time, and what do you see? You see a business plan! As God created the universe, so Jack Welch created the modern corporation. And he looked and saw that it was without boundaries: There was no border between him

THE COMIC (CONTINUED)

and his own corporate ends. Nothing tied him down—no restrictions, no regulations, no marriage vows. There was nothing between him and the object of desire. All growth, all the time, 24–7–365.

And where Jack Welch led, others soon followed. "No limits," crowed Showtime. "No boundaries," chimed Ford. Not mere sloganizing but a new faith, based on a new understanding of the cosmos. Of course CEOs don't want to be transparent—90% of the matter in the universe can't be seen. Sure CEOs inflated their earnings—the universe went through an inflationary period too. It's *still* expanding. What are you going to do, put the universe in jail?

"But hold on a moment!" my good friend opposing counsel will no doubt protest. What about the law of gravity? How is it possible that CEOs followed the logic of the big bang but not the law of gravity? I can answer that question in two words: quantum physics.

Before science made this quantum leap, a boundary was a straight line drawn down the middle of two things, like the line between "either" and "or." Either things were black, or they were white; either light was a wave, or it was a particle. But in the quantum world, light manifests as both a wave and a particle.

And as in the quantum world, so in the corporate world, where, as quantum expert George Bush recently declared, "Things aren't exactly black-and-white when it comes to accounting procedures." If brokers talk up stocks that they themselves are dumping, well, it's because in the financial world, things aren't exactly right or wrong. They can be both: The stock is simply good and bad—good for my clients, bad for you.

No, if a crime has been committed, it has been against these poor CEOs, men of business, men of science. As they stand before you now, empty shells of the giants they once were, I can only pray that there exists among you some shred of decency. And if indeed, as I suspect, there is ... my clients would like to buy it.

DISCUSSION QUESTIONS FOR SECTION 5

1. Do you believe the fundamental premise of the first article that women are more ethical managers than men? Explain your answer.

2. What characteristics of ethical leadership did Harry Kraemer of Baxter exhibit during its crisis discussed in the second article?

3. Who (other than your parents) would you list as important mentors in your life?

4. The final two articles are rather critical of CEOs. Do you agree with these authors' views? Why or why not?

BUSINESS ETHICS EARLY IN THE 21ST CENTURY

This section contains four articles that build upon the preceding material. Although determining what articles should conclude any readings book is always difficult, this task was particularly challenging since so many strong *Fast Company* articles exist. The first article focuses on businesses at the crossroads. The title seems particularly germane given the spate of recent scandals experienced throughout the U.S. business community. Five half-truths of business are examined. The first half-truth is refuted by the importance of integrity and self-respect in all business dealings. A second recognizes the stakeholder, rather than just the shareholder, model for guiding companies. The third half-truth pertains to leadership. Many times throughout this book we have emphasized the need for ethical rather than heroic leaders. The fourth half-truth encourages companies to think twice before laying off workers. This writer would stress the point made in the introductory section about moral imagination as a strategy in refuting this half-truth. Finally, the last half-truth discusses prosperity. Though many people are better off today then they were a decade ago due to capitalism's global triumph, a significant underclass exists not only in the United States, but throughout the world. The article admonishes CEOs to "rally around a new set of business truths." (In the original *Fast Company* article, the authors annotated the text with margin comments, including their initials. These comments are italicized and set in parentheses after the text to which they refer.)

The second article focuses attention on the issue of privacy in our Internet-based society. Several common-sense recommendations that would be useful in developing a privacy policy are offered for companies. The recommendations and a brief summary are as follows: Be up-front—it's better to be candid then coy; Stay in control—do not let third parties use your data to communicate with your customers; Show some restraint—limit the number of communications to consumers and respect users' privacy; Ask for permission—the concept of permission marketing is predicated on consumers opting-in; Pick a strategy—understand that not all consumers have the same view of privacy. On the last point, some consumers are more utilitarian (cost/benefit) in their view towards privacy, while others take a rights-based perspective.

The third article moves from the specific to the general. It features Professor Martha Nussbaum and her views on values. She is a well-known philosopher who also helps businesses develop their global values. In her seminar with business executives, Nussbaum poses the key question: What would a moral global system look like? "Her answer: the 'capabilities approach,' a set of universal values that includes the right to life, the right to bodily health and integrity, the right to participate in political affairs, and the right to hold property."

The final selection returns to a discussion of how September 11, 2001 affected people. The title of both the article and the book on which the interview is based is called "Good Work." All three co-authors are quoted in this article. They emphasize the importance of an individual focusing his life on what they call good work. In the article and book they discuss the "3M test": mission, model, and mirror. The mission pertains to how one wants to live her life. The modeling refers to people who are admired and respected. (Recall the earlier article on mentoring.) The mirror test, not surprisingly, occurs when a person looks at himself in the mirror and asks: Am I the kind of person I want to be?

Although not contained in the interview, ending this section overview with a few sentences from *Good Work* seemed appropriate. Two of this writer's most admired individuals are quoted, and their wish for you is my wish.

> All of us who believe in good work can find inspiration in what the anthropologist Margaret Mead said: "Never doubt that a small group of committed people can change the world. Indeed it is the only thing that ever has." And let's remember the way that Garrison Keillor signs off on the radio feature "Writer's Almanac"—"Be well, do good work, and keep in touch." (p. 249)

BY ROBERT SIMONS, HENRY MINTZBERG, AND KUNAL BASU

FROM *FAST COMPANY* ISSUE 59, PAGE 117

MEMO

To: CEOs
Re: Five Half-Truths of Business

BUSINESS IS AT A CROSSROADS. SCANDAL AND RECESSION HAVE CAST A PALL ON THE WAY CEOS GO ABOUT LEADING THEIR COMPANIES. THREE DISTINGUISHED PROFESSORS SEND THIS MEMO—FIVE HALF-TRUTHS OF BUSINESS—AS A WAKE-UP CALL.

Business is at a crossroads. Capitalism is facing a crisis. All of us who believe in business—from CEOs to business-school professors—must recognize that we have contributed to this crisis. The problem is simple, yet profound: We are all captives of five half-truths that shape the way we think about business and the way we do business. As a result, we may be in the process of destroying the very thing we cherish.

Enron. Andersen. Global Crossing. These business catastrophes are merely the tip of the black iceberg. Under the surface lies a culture that is increasingly defined by selfishness. To some extent, that is natural: We all want to succeed, to strive, to achieve. But carried to the extreme, the glorification of greed is causing a disconnect between the interests of the few and the well-being of the many. Consequently, the public's confidence in business and in large-scale institutions has been shaken.

Recovery is in the air. But so are feelings of deep distress on the part of anxious workers, a call for controls on the part of angry elected officials, and a palpable fear radiating from investors whose life savings may be at risk.

As business leaders and academics, we need to challenge what we do and what we teach. For some years now, we've been captured by a questionable set of beliefs—assumptions about business that are, at best, half-truths. Here, then, are the five half-truths of business.

1. We're only in it for ourselves. Think of this as the first law of business: In our finance classes, we are teaching a view of the world that says that each of us is obsessively self-interested and intent on maximizing personal gain. Economic Man, we tell our students, has one goal: more. And to get more, each of us is willing to do anything. *(In other words, there are no absolutes—not even integrity and self-respect.—RS)*

133

It is, of course, a half-truth. To some extent, we are all self-interested. And today, perhaps more than ever, there are plenty of people—business leaders, financiers, consultants, athletes, professors—who are willing to sell their integrity for a price. There are people who just want more and who are willing to do whatever it takes—and take whatever they can get.

But not everyone is self-interested all of the time, out for all that they can get. There are still CEOs who won't sacrifice long-term interests for short-term gains, financiers who walk away from unethical deals, consultants who level with their clients no matter what, athletes who won't endorse useless products, and professors who refuse to bend the truth as expert witnesses. These are people for whom integrity and self-respect are basic values—absolute needs—that are not open to negotiation. *(Where can we find role models? And how do we get their stories out?—HM)*

Beyond outer material goods lies an inner sense of good. Beyond calculation lies judgment. In fact, that is the essence of real leadership and responsible management: the ability to judge the difference between short-term calculable gains and deeply rooted core values.

But here's the problem: The half-truth of Economic Man drives a wedge of distrust into society. If we truly believe that each of us is nothing more than a calculator, then we become a society of calculations. Business simply won't work if each of us is only in it for ourselves. *(Communism toppled because of too little private interest; could capitalism be undermined by too much?—HM)* While we need to have individual initiative, we survive in a context of social engagement.

2. Corporations exist to maximize shareholder value.

If there is a mantra that CEOs today have learned to repeat almost mindlessly, this is it. Analysts, the media, and institutional stock traders rate, reprimand, and reward companies and their CEOs based on this single standard of performance.

What's remarkable about the current worship at the altar of shareholder value is that it's a reversal of our prior beliefs and behaviors. We used to say that corporations exist to serve society. After all, that was why they were originally granted charters— and why those charters could be revoked. We used to recognize corporations as both economic and social institutions—as organizations that were designed to serve a balanced set of stakeholders, not just the narrow economic interests of the shareholders. *(Do we really want to live in a society where corporations are accountable to no one but shareholders?—HM)*

In fact, for years, the CEOs of the 200 largest companies in the United States promoted this view most vocally. Your predecessors of the Business Roundtable regularly asserted a balanced philosophy of corporate responsibility. Here's what they wrote in their statement on corporate responsibility from 1981: "Balancing the shareholder's expectations of maximum return against other priorities is one of the fundamental problems confronting corporate management. The shareholder must receive a good return but the legitimate concerns of other constituencies (customers, employees, communities, suppliers, and society at large) also must have the appropriate attention."

Then, in 1997, the Business Roundtable announced that it was making a remarkable U-turn. *(How could CEOs who signed this think they are leaders?—RS)* Its report on corporate governance assigned a new priority to CEOs: Maximize shareholder value. "The notion that the board must somehow balance the interests of stockholders against the interests of other stakeholders fundamentally misconstrues the role of directors," the report read. "It is, moreover, an unworkable notion because it would leave the board with no criterion for resolving conflicts between interests of stockholders and of other stakeholders or among different groups of stakeholders."

Here's what that statement actually means: When it comes right down to it, the customer may be king and the employees may be the corporation's greatest asset. But the CEO's only real responsibility is to serve the interests of the shareholders.

Now let's take a look at who these shareholders are, what they own, and how they own it. The way that the economy works today, with instantaneous information, global capital flows, and Internet-based stock trading, fewer and fewer shareholders are genuinely committed in any way to the companies that they "own." Giant mutual funds buy and sell millions of shares each day to mirror impersonal market indexes. Programs instruct traders on which shares to buy or sell and when—although rarely on why. Then there are the recently arrived day traders, who become shareholders of a company and then ex-shareholders of that company within a matter of hours, as they surf the market for momentum plays or arbitrage opportunities. These are the shareholders—who may not have any interest in the company's products, services, employees, or customers—whose interests you are now pledged to maximize.

Of course, there is a half-truth in this mantra: Shareholders' interests are significant. The capital markets do need to work, and for that, shareholders need a fair return on their investment. But there is a larger truth to this half-truth: Maximizing shareholder value at the expense of all of the other stakeholders is bad for business and bad for capitalism. It drives a wedge between those who create the economic value—the employees—and those who harvest its benefits. Customers, too, recognize the cynicism of a company that only sees them as dollar signs. *(Imagine a company that puts its shareholders first—only to discover that it has alienated its customers!—RS)* That may be one reason why the American Customer Satisfaction Index has declined steadily in almost every industry since the mid-1990s. "Maximize shareholder value" may be the job description that CEOs automatically recite —but it is profoundly misguided.

3. Companies need CEOs who are heroic leaders. This is another half-truth. Of course, one of the CEO's roles is to provide leadership. But the real question is, what kind of leadership?

The notion of the CEO as heroic leader is one that you've heard so often that you've probably come to believe it: The CEO is the company, a heroic leader who single-handedly steers the business to success. *(Real heroes are those who encourage others to act heroically. Leaders make more leaders.—HM)*

Two questions are worth asking: Why did this half-truth emerge? And how did it happen? In large part, the "why" is a reflection of half-truth number two. Having heroic CEOs serves the interests of the shareholders, who want disproportionate rewards. How did they bring this notion into practice? In simple terms, you CEOs were bought. All it took were huge bonuses and excessive stock options!

The fig leaf that covered those rewards was an equally large set of assumptions. The business world was led to believe that you, the CEO, are the embodiment of the company, that you alone are responsible for the company's entire performance, that your performance can be measured, and that the one important measurement is the creation of shareholder value. And all it took to validate those assumptions was the creation of heroic, larger-than-life CEOs. Taking the cue, business journalists happily provided personalities and simple explanations to fit the bill. CEOs became celebrities. One example: In its April 14, 1997 issue, Fortune magazine wrote of IBM CEO Louis Gerstner, "In four years Gerstner has added more than $40 billion to IBM's market value." Admittedly, Lou Gerstner is an excellent CEO. But did he really do that all by himself?

The problem with the notion of heroic leadership, of course, is not just that it's preposterous on the face of it. It is also corrosive to the connection that needs to exist between a real leader and the people who make the company work. *(The problem is, we've put leaders on a pedestal. Everyone else is just looking on.—HM)* Real leadership is connected, involved, and engaged. It's often more quiet than heroic. Real leadership is about teamwork, about taking a long-term view, about building an organization slowly, carefully, and collectively. As CEOs, your job is to set an example of energizing others, not to take dramatic actions that let you take the lion's share of the spoils.

Nothing reveals the corruption of leadership more clearly than the record of executive compensation. According to one recent survey of executive compensation during the 1990s, your pay rose by 570%. Profits rose by 114%. Average worker pay rose 37%, barely ahead of inflation, which went up by 32%. In 1999, while median shareholders' returns fell by 3.9%, CEO direct compensation rose another 10.8%. *(We all went along with this because CEOs told workers that they'd get stock options too!—RS)* Perhaps the real reason that we are so obsessed with leadership today is that we see so little of it from CEOs.

4. Companies need to be lean and mean. "Lean and mean" is back in fashion these days. It's a mantra for getting in shape after the recession, just in time for the recovery. "Lean" certainly sounds good—better than "fat." But the fact that "mean" sounds good is a sad sign of the times.

There is nothing clever about firing large numbers of people. CEOs who have pursued slash-and-burn tactics—the fastest way to create shareholder value!—have produced companies that are skinny and just plain mean. "Chainsaw" Al Dunlap, the master of slash and burn (who eventually slashed-and-burned himself), wasn't an aberration; he was an extreme example of a popular trend. In 2000, before the recession even hit, employers cut 1.2 million workers, ending the year with the highest number of layoffs since the Bureau of Labor Statistics resumed calculating them in 1995.

Of course, lean and mean offers the same half-promises as the other half-truths: Embrace it, and you'll get lower costs, higher productivity, flatter structures, empowered workers, and delighted customers! *(Downsizing isn't a strategy—it's a cop-out!—HM)* You'll get—in those glib phrases of the day—"more for less" and a "win win" situation.

Well, maybe. Or maybe you'll get burned-out managers, angry workers, quality losses under the guise of productivity gains, and bad service that alienates customers. In other words, you'll get "less for less" and a "lose lose" situation.

But the biggest loss of all may be the sense of betrayal that workers have come to feel toward their employers. *(The pledge of job security in exchange for loyalty has been thrown out the window.—RS)* One recent study reported that only 34% of employees worldwide felt a strong sense of loyalty to their employers. In the United States, only 47% of employees saw the leaders of their companies as people of high personal integrity. And that was before Enron, Andersen, or Global Crossing. In other words, that was before some of your fellow CEOs gave their workers more evidence that they were right to be distrustful.

5. A rising tide lifts all boats. This last half-truth helps knit together the first four. In order for the focus on personal gain, shareholder value, heroic management, and lean and increasingly mean organizations to work, we must find a way to rationalize what otherwise looks like self-serving behavior. The solution: "A rising tide lifts all boats" fits.

It's hard to argue against prosperity. And we'd all rather see the economy flowing rather than ebbing. But even as a metaphor, the idea that a rising tide lifts all boats doesn't hold water. What we've really been observing is a tidal wave. If you've ever lived along a coastline, then you know that a tidal wave lifts only those boats that aren't moored to anything. The boats that are connected to real things get swamped. For those who live on land, a tidal wave can turn into a flood. The ordinary folks who live in the lowlands get flooded out, while the wealthy few who live in high places escape. So much for the "win win" benefits.

But what about the facts of business and economics? In 1989, there were 66 billionaires and 31.5 million people in the United States living below the official poverty line. In 1999, the number of billionaires had increased to 268—and the number of people living below the poverty line had increased to 34.5 million. *(What we're seeing is a growing disparity between the rich and the poor, the haves and the have-nots.—RS)* A recent UN survey of the world's wealthiest countries ranked the United States highest both in gross domestic product and in poverty rates.

And what about the stock market and all of the shareholder value that you helped create? Here again, the rising tide only lifted the yachts. Between 1989 and 1998, the wealthiest 10% of American households saw their stock-market holdings increase by more than 72%, while those in the bottom 60% saw their holdings increase by less than 4%. Yes, stock ownership has been up by about 16% during the past 10 years. But more than 50% of all Americans don't own stocks or mutual funds, and only 33% of all households with stocks have holdings worth $5,000 or more. The bottom line: In 1999, at the height of a decade long economic boom, one in six American children was officially poor, and 26% of the workforce was subsisting on poverty-level wages. *(This is absolutely shocking. Imagine a family of three* *living on an annual income of $13,000. Poverty like this threatens our future.—RS)* More than 30% of U.S. households have a net worth (including homes and investments) of less than $10,000.

Of course, we can all take pride in capitalism's global triumph over communism and in its spread around the world. Or can we? The recent backlash against globalization is due in no small part to the promises that capitalism hasn't kept to poor people in poor countries—those whose boats have not been lifted. In some countries in South America and Africa, the top 20% of the population gets more than 60% of the nation's income, while the bottom 10% of the population gets less than 1%.

Business—and capitalism—are at a crossroads. Newspaper headlines today suggest a gathering crisis, one of performance, values, and confidence. It's time for CEOs to rally around a new set of business truths. *(If you're as concerned as we are, visit our Web site and forward this article to other leaders (www.fastcompany.com/keyword/ceos52).—RS)* It's time for an agenda that restores faith in business, trust in business leaders, and hope in the future.

Contact Robert Simons (simons@hbs.edu), Henry Mintzberg (mintzber@management.mcgill.ca), and Kunal Basu (kunal.basu@templeton.oxford.ac.uk) by email. Find a longer draft of this memo on the Web (http://www.henrymintzberg.com).

BY GEORGE ANDERS   FROM *FAST COMPANY* ISSUE 47, PAGE 186

Can You Keep a Secret?

THE PUSH FOR ONLINE PRIVACY THREATENS TO KILL THE DREAM OF SUPER-SOPHISTICATED, NET-DRIVEN MARKETING. BUT THERE ARE SIMPLE WAYS THAT COMPANIES CAN HAVE THEIR DATA AND PROTECT IT TOO.

At the height of the internet boom, marketers had big dreams about harnessing the power of consumer information. As they saw it, the Internet had created opportunities for data mining, cross-selling, and targeted marketing that went far beyond what was feasible in traditional commerce. Airlines could find out who was checking fares to the Caribbean. Health-care companies could keep track of who was reading up on diabetes or schizophrenia. At last, it would be fast, easy, and cheap to profile a vast assortment of customers—and to pitch them accordingly.

But then the privacy backlash set in. Consumers began to worry that their health records, their music tastes, and other information about them were being put at the disposal of strangers. Meanwhile, a highly vocal privacy-advocacy community began publicizing outrage-of-the-month incidents—which put pressure on perceived offenders to back away from plans to make full use of customer data. Amazon.com, for example, tried to publish lists of the books that sold best among employees of Coca-Cola, IBM, and the like, only to retreat after some customers complained that their reading tastes weren't anyone else's business.

As a result, lots of big companies began treating online privacy in a purely defensive way—as an issue to be handled mainly by their legal department. "Just don't get it wrong" supplanted "Get it right."

Lately, though, all sorts of organizations that do business on the Internet are taking a fresh look at their privacy strategies. Their objective: to strike the right balance between shielding each user's privacy and exploiting a rich mountain of consumer data. "Good privacy can be a good business practice," contends David Kramer, a partner at Wilson Sonsini Goodrich & Rosati, one of Silicon Valley's top law firms. "If you think about it, it's really part of good customer service."

In this new environment, companies aren't abandoning efforts to extract value from online databases. But they are gathering and exploiting data in a more consumer-sensitive way. Replacing the strip-mining tactics that consumers fear most is an approach that rests on a few basic principles.

BE UP-FRONT

Over the past few years, companies have tended to keep privacy issues in a haze. Too often, privacy policies have been verbose and jargon-filled, and companies have buried them in obscure corners of Web sites or deep inside long-winded emails.

That's not smart, and in some industries, it's not even legal. New federal regulations require companies in the health-care and financial-services fields to post clear highly visible privacy policies on the Web, and to remind users repeatedly that they can opt out of future marketing initiatives. But even in industries where anything goes, there's a strong case to be made for being candid rather than coy. If you want your customers to remain your customers, then you should be reasonably clear about how you plan to use information about them—and what their rights are regarding that information.

Isn't there a risk that most consumers will make their data off-limits if the opt-out card is easy to play? Not if companies convince consumers that data sharing is worth it. In fact, if opt-out rates start to rise much above 10%, that's probably a good sign that a company has done a poor job of designing its marketing promotions.

STAY IN CONTROL

Don't let a third party use your data to communicate directly with customers. That's a steady refrain of Marc Loewenthal, chief privacy officer at Providian Financial, a San Francisco-based credit-card issuer. Sure, there are good reasons why Providian might allow businesses like Avis Rent A Car, Flowers.com, and Marriott Hotels to pitch their goodies to its online customers. But, Loewenthal says, that kind of dialogue should always begin with an email or targeted ad sent by Providian itself, and only those customers who respond to such a message should be put in touch with a third-party marketer.

From a privacy standpoint, Loewenthal argues, that's a much more attractive option than opening up vast swathes of Providian's cardholder registry to outsiders. Customers receive only those pitches that Providian thinks might appeal to them—and they don't run the risk of getting bombarded with spam. What's more, Providian maximizes the long-term value of its large customer database. "That's a no-brainer for us," Loewenthal says. "Customer data is very valuable to us, and we need to guard it very jealously."

SHOW SOME RESTRAINT

An energetic marketing department can conjure up dozens of online cross-marketing opportunities every month. Did you use the Web to buy a tent? Then surely you'd be a good candidate for lots of targeted email about camping getaways. Given that mass emails to customers are essentially free, it's tempting to deluge customers with promotional messages.

But smart marketers know that a profusion of pitches can be downright annoying—whether those pitches come in the form of emails or of telemarketing calls at dinnertime. "We try to limit our communications to one per month," says Sue deLeeuw, head of brand management at NextCard Inc., an online credit-card issuer in San Francisco. "That's about as much as people want to hear."

In the past year, otherwise well-respected Internet merchants like Amazon.com and CDNow.com have begun to strain customers' tolerance by pestering them with too many "special offers" that just aren't very special. DeLeeuw's advice: Focus on sending users pitches that are truly valuable and few in number. Beyond that, respect users' privacy and leave them alone.

ASK FOR PERMISSION

Marketing mavericks like Fast Company columnist Seth Godin have argued for years that it's wasteful to beam a message to large masses of online users. Godin has advocated a "permission marketing" approach in which companies contact only users who demonstrate an interest in being courted. (See "Permission Marketing," April: May 1998.) So far, that's been a hard concept for most big companies to embrace. But more and more industry leaders contend that customer data should be made available to marketers only if customers say so.

"I've become a big believer in opt-in strategies," says Sandra England, president of PGP Security, a unit of Santa Clara, California-based Network Associates. "You get greater stability over your customer base. Instead of waiting to see who says no, you can create incentives for people to check the 'yes' box."

Of course, the opt-in approach has a downside. Companies that have experimented with it say that 10% to 40% of users choose to share their data—which is well below the 90% to 95% of users whose data typically becomes available through an opt-out approach. But a lower response rate isn't necessarily bad. If your goal is to sell a sophisticated product, such as a high-end computer server or microchip, then an opt-in strategy may be a good way to target the natural buyers of that item.

PICK A STRATEGY

When it comes to privacy, consumers don't all want the same thing. A recent Harris Interactive-Wall Street Journal poll revealed an intriguing split in Internet users' attitudes toward privacy. Roughly one-quarter (24%) of respondents were "very concerned" about threats to their personal privacy on the Internet. But another quarter (27%) voiced little or no unease. (The rest fell somewhere in the middle.) That schism suggests that industry rivals may thrive by adopting contrasting privacy strategies.

A notable test case comes in the consumer market for Internet service. America Online greets its users with a cornucopia of marketing offers every time they log on to the service. Sure, AOL provides basic privacy safeguards, but if you're looking for seclusion on the Internet, this is not the service for you. By contrast, smaller ISPs don't attract nearly as much interest from marketers. So either by necessity or by design, companies like EarthLink are trying to woo users who want more privacy and less chatter.

It may take years to know which strategy works best, but either choice may be better than trying to occupy some ill-defined middle ground. The key is to calibrate your privacy policies to the privacy expectations of customers in your target market. In any case, it's much too soon to give up on the dream of using the Net to reach those customers.

George Anders (ganders@fastcompany.com), a *Fast Company* senior editor, is based in Silicon Valley.

BY HARRIET RUBIN   FROM *FAST COMPANY* ISSUE 60, PAGE 118

Global Values in a Local World

MEET MARTHA NUSSBAUM, ONE OF AMERICA'S LEADING PHILOSOPHERS. SHE'S ASKING SOME TOP BUSINESSPEOPLE TO CONFRONT TODAY'S TOUGHEST QUESTION: ARE THERE GLOBAL VALUES TO CONNECT US ALL?

The Microsoft lawyer is choking back tears. The CEO of a multinational food company is pacing about in mourner's clothes. The dean of a business school is assessing the harm he has caused to a lawyer from Tanzania, whose daughter he has murdered.

Into this mess strides the sheriff of the new world order: Martha Craven Nussbaum. At 55, she is America's foremost philosopher, a title retired since Ralph Waldo Emerson died in 1882. Nussbaum is halfway into a weeklong seminar whose purpose is to teach business leaders how to think about "Core Values for a Global Society." The class's immediate assignment: to stage The Trojan Women, the ancient Greek play whose main character, Hecuba, the queen, finds her homeland conquered in war by the Greek army. Think of it as an encounter with terrorists. All of the things that define Hecuba—her title, her freedom, her luxuries, even her children—are gone in an instant. Who is she, deep down, minus every shred of her title and her identity? And here's a question for the class—and the rest of us—to ponder: Is there any part of us that is safe from the whims of fate?

The timing of this production is almost scary: It is mid-August—one year ago. Twelve leaders from various backgrounds attend an executive seminar sponsored by the Aspen Institute, where they're learning about the human core that unites people. The idea is for them to act out destruction and evil to get a sense of its reality, its costs, and, strangely, its opportunities. Just three weeks later, on September 11, this fiction will collide with reality. Three weeks later, we will know Hecuba better than her own neighbors did. Three weeks later, we will be wrestling with the new questions that confront a world that has suddenly changed its shape: Is there a global set of values that inform us all? Are we all part of a shrinking world where we can count on our commonalities to keep the whole ball of wax in one piece? Or has the world suddenly lost its commonalities and its common sense? Is it a stranger, more disconnected place?

"The Greeks show us how in agony we learn wisdom: The fullness of life is in the hazards of life," Nussbaum tells her students. "A safe life is not worth living." After September 11, it's said, the world that was getting smaller suddenly got larger. Now it's impossible to buy the world a Coke—or even to know for sure what the

143

stranger next to you is thinking. American values, marked by American commerce, hardly seem to offer a single global standard. In fact, defining "core values" seems a distinctly unfashionable inquiry now that diversity and local interests have donned a dangerous face.

It may also be that the search for core values constitutes our last, best hope of sanity. For five days, these 12 leaders who could have been dipping their toes in the sand are instead studying how leadership can take global aim. They have come together with the belief that business deserves the credit for many of the glories of the world—but that it also must lay equal claim to its messes.

These students believe that the mission of shaping the world's future is too important to be left to politicians. It is their task to discover a definition of the good life—one on which all societies can agree. And to search for that answer is to ask a harder question: If we can't agree, is survival in this powder-keg world possible?

"If you really push people," says Nussbaum, speaking to the class, "they'll agree that virtue is more important than money. What virtue means to people whose interests are as different as women from men, young from old, rich from poor—that is what we're trying to understand."

Hecuba, it turns out, holds a key. "A condition of being good is that it should always be possible for you to be morally destroyed by something that you couldn't prevent," says Nussbaum. "To be a good human being is to have a kind of openness to the world, an ability to trust uncertain things beyond your own control, things that can lead you to be shattered in very extreme circumstances for which you were not to blame. That says something very important about the ethical life: It is based on a trust in the uncertain and on a willingness to be exposed. Trust is based on being more like a plant than like a jewel—something fragile but whose very particular beauty is inseparable from that fragility."

At the heart of the inquiry into values is a quest for a working definition of leadership—which, it begins to emerge in the class discussion, is the unique gift of philosophy. Reading great works of philosophy, Nussbaum says, develops an important—and often overlooked—element of yourself: These stories make demands on us to be internal critics. "If we made this demand on ourselves more readily, we'd make it on our public figures," she explains. "We would insist that they play the role of gadfly within the system."

Leaders have been wrestling with core values since the Greeks invented the idea of the good life as something that only organizations can provide. Rational thought, they argued, can settle any dispute. After all, everyone is human, so, of course, everyone wants the same things.

But that was only true as long as "everyone" was a free Greek citizen. History reveals a long and troubled conflict about core values. Christianity dominated much of Europe and beyond in the early Middle Ages, but by 715, nascent Islam had taken hold of areas south and east of the Mediterranean, and even most of Spain. With little warning, the world order had changed. And the new challenger carried an entirely different sense of how things did—or should—work. In the back-and-forth of conflict, core values were unheard of. Beliefs and values not only conflicted, they also called for battle. Looked at one way, history is the story of people who seem happier to be defined by their differences than to be joined by what they share.

In fact, on the next to last day of the seminar, the differences erupt into the open. Fatma A. Karume, a lawyer from Tanzania, is sick of white, Western people telling her—"telling Africa"—what to do. She speaks with the voice of the Muslim world that wants an end to the American Empire and globalization. Tom Swartele, the CEO of North American operations for Bongrain SA, the multinational food conglomerate, is the beneficiary of cultural dissension. Growing up in Belgium, Swartele initially spoke only Dutch. But in a country where Flemmish and French cultures compete, he became fluent in both languages—which ultimately has brought him more opportunities. His wealth and stature are a result.

Nussbaum has been waiting for this melee, for the moment when the class would display the kind of chaos that's loose in the world. She then asks the key question: "What would a moral global system look like? A United States of the World? How does one get there? How is one to think?"

Her answer: the "capabilities approach," a set of universal values that includes the right to life, the right to bodily health and integrity, the right to participate in political affairs, and the right to hold property. "We reasonably disagree about many matters," Nussbaum says. "That is why freedom of religion and freedom of speech and association are so very important. Each person ought to search for the meaning of life in his or her own way, using the resources of whatever religious or philosophical tradition he or she likes. For political purposes, we can also agree to endorse a common core of basic principles of justice. But I do not think that political philosophers should be in the business of recommending a fully comprehensive account of the human good, because that would suggest disrespect for religion."

In the end, Nussbaum says, people risk their lives for justice every day. Justice is a form of love—and that is the emotion at the core of all values. "We have to love people and things outside our own will," she says, "and this means that we have to have fear, hope, and grief."

As we approach the one-year mark of America's greatest modern tragedy, it's worth remembering Nussbaum's admonition: "We begin our lives ... loving our parents, fearing their departure, angry at our inability to command fully the things that we need. In these weaknesses we find the strength of our relation to the world"—and to each other.

Harriet Rubin (hrubin@fastcompany.com) is a *Fast Company* senior writer.

Good Work

THE CORE MESSAGE OF OUR WHO'S FAST ISSUE IS THE POWER OF GOOD WORK. NOW THREE EMINENT PSYCHOLOGISTS ARE OUT WITH A NEW BOOK ACTUALLY CALLED "GOOD WORK." IN AN IN-DEPTH DISCUSSION, THEY DISCUSS THE RIGHT WAY TO THINK ABOUT YOUR PROFESSION AND CAREER.

Over the past four years, in our annual Who's Fast issue, Fast Company has profiled more than 50 leaders from all walks of life and all parts of the world. But there's been one core message behind these varied stories: Ordinary people with enough brains, passion, and conviction can achieve truly extraordinary results. The most powerful force in business isn't money or technology or naked ambition—it's a commitment to doing good work.

Enter now three eminent academic psychologists whose important and compelling new book makes much the same point. The title says it all: Good Work: When Excellence and Ethics Meet (Basic Books, 2001). The book, written by Harvard University professor Howard Gardner, Stanford University professor William Damon, and professor Mihaly Csikszentmihalyi of the Drucker School of Management at Claremont Graduate University, testifies to the power of a commitment to professional excellence and to the challenges of meeting those commitments in the face of fierce marketplace pressures.

Of course, September 11 and its aftermath have raised the issue of good work to even greater prominence. Suddenly, all of us want to feel that what we do actually means something. But doing that seems harder than ever, what with a society gripped by uncertainty, an economy gripped by recession, and each of us struggling as individuals to make sense of what's happening.

In an exclusive panel discussion, the authors of Good Work offer ideas and advice to help you stay focused on your work.

The horror of September 11 has our readers asking themselves tough questions: In a world shattered by terror and death, what genuinely matters? In the face of so much heroism and sacrifice, how do I make sense of what I do for a living? Whose contributions truly count? What are the valid sources of satisfaction and pride in terms of work? My question to you is, What does good work mean in light of these sorts of questions?

William Damon: In every conversation I've had since September 11, in almost any context, people have asked, What meaning does my work have now? And unless you're in the military or one of the security forces, it's not always easy to make a connection to this kind of cataclysmic event. But what we are trying to say is that anybody who's doing work—whether it's in law, medicine, journalism, engineering—needs to get in touch with the original mission of their field, the reason that profession was developed to begin with. Because all of those professions serve a public interest, and individuals who go into those fields originally have a clear sense of that, which why people speak about having a sense of a calling in life.

The problem is that all too often, such a sense of calling diminishes over the years as you get caught up in the kinds of career incentives that move people on a day-to-day basis—especially when those incentives pull people in the wrong direction, as they frequently do. For example, a lot of journalism these days is driven by sensationalism or work that's written so briefly and out of context that you don't really get the story across. Those practices pull you away from the mission of giving people information they need to live good lives and to support a democracy—the classic issues and missions of the field.

We're trying to show people a way to get in touch with the fundamental purpose and mission of the field they're working in, and to overcome the sense that to survive or to have a good career, you've got to compromise, you've got to cut corners, you've got to go along to get along. We think that's bad advice. We're trying to give examples of people who have become highly successful by being purposeful, by being ethical, by doing it the right way.

Howard Gardner: September 11 was a wake-up call. We often call our project "Good Work in Turbulent Times" to capture just that sentiment—although we didn't quite imagine how turbulent the times would be. There really are three different kinds of wake-up calls. One wake-up call is the individual wake-up call—like Saul on the road to Damascus—where something happens in your own life. You lose something, or you get fired, and it throws you back to the fundamentals of your field.

The second one is a wake-up call for the profession itself. The picture that Bill portrayed of journalism—where journalists still have ideals, but they feel that the conditions of work make it impossible to achieve those ideals—is a wake-up call for the profession.

But the third kind of wake-up call, which none of us had in mind at all while writing the book, is a societal wake-up call. All of a sudden, the assumptions that we've all been making about what human beings are like, and about America's place in the world, have been ripped to shreds. So we're now experiencing a kind of a triple wake-up call.

Mihaly Csikszentmihalyi: These wake-up calls are typically the moments when people think again about questions that are easy to ignore: What do I want to be remembered for? and What should I do so that I don't look back on my life and think it was wasted? It's too bad that as human beings, we address these questions only when things force them to our attention—like when we lose a loved one or our business is going down the drain or we face the kind of societal challenge we are now.

But, in some ways, of course, this is the moment when we have a choice to revisit the fundamental values that most of us have learned from our parents and our culture. Over time, evolution does select certain values as being necessary for our civil society to survive. We take them for granted, as we take good weather for granted and good air for granted. But when we see them threatened, we have to ask ourselves, what is it that makes life worth living? We are now in that position, and I hope we come up with a good answer.

Those are tough questions to ask, let alone to begin to know how to answer.

Howard Gardner: How's this for something simple? We propose the "3M test": mission, model, mirror. Mission is what we've been talking about until now. What's the core thing that you're trying to do in your work life? To make sure that poor people get justice, to make sure that people get well or get educated, to design excellent and beautiful products? There is a value core to every profession.

Number two is modeling. Whom do you admire? Whom would you would like to emulate? Who are the antimentors, the tormentors, the people who really give what you do a bad name? In journalism, we might talk about an Edward R. Murrow as opposed to a Matt Drudge, although I don't feel the need to single out poor Drudge.

The third thing is the mirror test, where you look at yourself in the mirror and you say, "Am I the kind of person I want to be?" Am I proud or embarrassed at looking at myself?

And then try what I call the "M2 test." If everybody in my field were behaving the way I am, would I feel proud about the profession, or would I feel ashamed? Compare journalism, say, in the Gary Condit era to journalism in the September 11 era. The Gary Condit era really showed us journalism at its worst.

William Damon: Let me give you a direct example of something that gets to what you are asking about. I was at a conference of academic psychologists shortly after September 11. Right from the beginning, a lot of people were saying, "Why did I even get into this field to begin with? What do we contribute? I feel that my work is so out of touch with the things that are really important when an incident like this happens."

And the fact is that the kinds of psychology these people were talking about were indeed dry, irrelevant to most concerns, and highly academic in the worst sense. They should have been asking themselves those questions all along, because just as their work wasn't relevant to a September 11, it was not relevant to the way any of us live our lives or to the things we care about. These people were doing studies for the sake of studies, studies for the sake of getting tenure at universities. This incredibly intelligent group of people could have been contributing so much more.

In every realm, if you value our civilization, if you value our public life, if you value the good things in our life, most professions have the potential to contribute to the public good and to civilization. But for that to happen, you have to orient people around the right questions, the right tests. You have to say, "What am I here for? What kind of a person do I want to be? Do I want to do the right thing? Or do I really just want to do what advances my career in the short term?" Eventually, it all comes down to aligning your day-to-day efforts with a sense of purpose that lets you contribute to the world.

Another big question people are facing is how do we move on? How do we turn off CNN and get back to work? What's your advice?

Mihaly Csikszentmihalyi: I think that getting immersed in an activity that provides you with feedback is always a good strategy. It's a good kind of antidote to looking at the future with fear. If you are really involved in something, whether it's a job or a relationship or a hobby, it will get your mind away from those things and make you feel better. But it also can become also a kind of escape unless you stop and take seriously the issues we have been talking about. The ideal situation is when you can experience this flow, this total involvement, within the context of an activity that is actually of value to society.

William Damon: That last point is really important. Of course, people in the past have tried to talk about the moral dimension to work and life. Every business school has some course on ethics. But what we're emphasizing is that the moral dimension doesn't have to be a trade-off. It doesn't have to be something that you do grudgingly; you don't have to view it as something that takes away from your success, that cuts down on the chances you'll make a lot of money, or that limits you from being highly esteemed in your field.

Our point is that if you approach things the right way, these two things actually enhance one another. The people with the really powerful careers are people who also tend to have a very elevated sense of purpose, who don't cut corners, who have a lot of integrity. They're not saints, and it's not that they never make mistakes, or that they've never taken a low road. Nobody is perfect. But, in the long run, these are people who tend to take the high road. The high road is the best road to success.

Polly LaBarre (plabarre@fastcompany.com) is a *Fast Company* senior editor.

DISCUSSION QUESTIONS FOR SECTION 6

1. Which of the five half-truths discussed in the first article has the most relevance to business ethics? Why?

2. Check the privacy policy on one of your favorite Web sites. How many of the principles examined in the second article does the company seem to follow?

3. Do you think that Professor Nussbaum's view on global values can be implemented by multinational organizations? Why or Why not?

4. What is your definition of "good work?" Compare it with the definitions of your classmates. Are there major differences?